D1029397

Homecomings

Wirline Morris

W Dudley

*For Andre Emmerich —
With much thanks for the
hospitality and tour at
Top Gallant —
my best —
Bill Dudley
Fall '92*

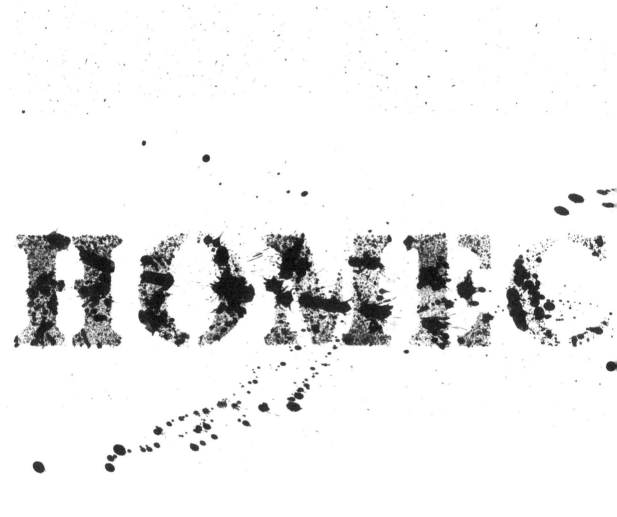

Author and Artist Series

University Press of Mississippi
Jackson & London

by Willie Morris
with the art of William Dunlap

Text copyright © 1989 by Willie Morris
Art copyright © 1989 by William Dunlap
Introduction copyright © 1989 by the
University Press of Mississippi

Manufactured in the United States of America
93 92 91 90   5 4 3 2
Designed by John A. Langston

Lettering on title page and chapter openings by
William Dunlap

"Capote Remembered" appeared in a slightly different version in *Southern Magazine*.
"A Return to Christmases Gone" appeared in *Mississippi* Magazine.

Library of Congress Cataloging-in-Publication Data

Morris, Willie.
  Homecomings.

  (Author and artist series)
  1. Morris, Willie—Biography. 2. Authors, Ameri-
can—20th century—Biography. 3. Mississippi—So-
cial life and customs. I. Dunlap, William, 1944–
  . II. Title. III. Series.
PS3563.087452467 1989   814'.54   89-16683
ISBN 0-87805-416-2
ISBN 0-87805-417-0 (lim. ed.)

British Library Cataloguing in Publication data
available.

to Dr. Verner Holmes of McComb and
downtown Lexie, to Vern Holmes of
the Bogue Chitto, and to Susanne Dietzel
and Dave R.—whose friendship runs deep
as the Bogue Chitto itself.

Color plates follow page 30

Dialogue:
The Author and the Artist

Willie Morris lives in Oxford, Mississippi. One late afternoon in summer 1989 his friend, the painter William Dunlap, of McLean, Virginia, stopped by for a visit. The two men, both native Mississippians, talked about things that matter to them—language and the land and memory, shared experiences, and homecomings. This is an excerpt from their conversation.

MORRIS: Bill, how long have you been living permanently away from this state?

DUNLAP: I got out of Ole Miss in '69 and was on the faculty one year at Hinds Junior College, and then my old ex-professors here at Ole Miss beckoned me to come to the mountains of North Carolina. That was the sort of opportunity one couldn't turn down. So, I "coached" art at Appalachian State University for ten years. I've lived away from Mississippi since 1971, but I've never really been out of this place.

MORRIS: Well, I know.

DUNLAP: And I've rather fastidiously planned my homecoming. I've bought the old Starnes house up in Webster County right across the pasture from Mother's place. It's a fine old 1907 carpenter Gothic frame house full of mission furniture. It's been the subject of countless paintings.

MORRIS: Didn't you tell me it's an old church?

DUNLAP: There's a defunct Church of Christ on the property that I'm turning into a studio. Highway 82 runs between the church and the house, and they've been threatening to widen it since I was a kid or before. *Now* the Mississippi Highway Department is about to do it. I saw the surveyor's stakes just yesterday when I was by Mother's house. The right-of-way for the new Highway 82 is going to come right through the middle of my sanctuary, and it breaks my heart.

MORRIS: Running it through the house? The kitchen?

DUNLAP: Well, no, the house is safe; it's the studio, which is crucial to my coming home and making art, that will be affected. I've got to have a place to work, and the church studio conversion is already underway. I've got the lights right, walls and storage areas built, and the Jacuzzi man was coming over from Winona to turn the baptistry into a place where the spirit can really move you! And now I guess I'll have to push the building back a hundred yards or so. It's going to be a considerable disruption. My heart's just gone out of it.

MORRIS: You're going to move back here permanently?

DUNLAP: No, but I would like to be here several months out of the year, in the fall and spring certainly. My wife Linda [Burgess] has a studio in New York, I'm in Washington, so it makes sense to have a place on neutral ground. We can work wherever we are.

Speaking of moving, Willie, this is something I've got to confess to you. I'm haunting some of your old caverns up in New York. The people there hear me talk, and Mississippi comes up, and the first thing some of these folks want to know: "Do you know Willie? Have you seen Willie? How's Willie?" These "Willie watchers" are ubiquitous. And I'm always proud to report that you're the eye of a literary storm down here in Lafayette County that is, in fact, a renaissance.

Willie, I remember when I was in college and you were in New York at *Harper's,* you came down to the Old Capitol for some occasion and gave a wonderful talk. You stood behind the rostrum there where your ancestors—grandfathers, great-grandfathers—had spoken, and you talked about this place. It was very moving for me. I was looking for permission to be an artist in Mississippi. And people like you in the flesh and Miss Welty and the knowledge of Mr. Faulkner granted me a kind of permission to be what I wanted to be before I really even knew what an artist was.

MORRIS: Well, buddy, I'm happy to take some of the credit. I'm a great admirer of your paintings, which I sometimes think of as visual poems. Do you ever think of them that way?

DUNLAP: Certainly. I'll accept that. I grew up in what some of my erudite and more sophisticated friends would call a vacuum. There were no museums where I was growing up, no galleries, and no painters that I knew on a first-hand basis. But what there was was a great concentration of another kind of spirit: there was this extraordinary landscape that one could see.

On my drive up today from Greenwood I counted no fewer than nine different shades of green. Great effects of atmospheric perspective out there that I just grew up always seeing. I think it's true that, with some, one sense overrides the others—be it touch, smell, or hearing. Someone with a good ear becomes a musician. Whatever the visual equivalent of perfect pitch is, I like to think, drove me to look at the world around me and to draw it obsessively. I always drew, and I was encouraged to do

xi

Dialogue

it. I haven't so much become an artist in spite of the fact that I grew up without museums but, I think, because of it. There was a vacuum that I needed to fill for myself.

MORRIS: I think there are parallels between the kind of work you and I do. Growing up in Yazoo City, that small town on the edge of the Delta, we were very isolated, and before the horrendous television culture, I was suffused with words all around me, people telling stories and telling them with immense flamboyance and sorrow, graphic stories. And as you said, there was the landscape—the nine shades of green everywhere, the kudzu vines, the flat land. The whole phenomenon of memory and how memory relates to the landscape itself and to the people around you, I think, probably pushed me along as a writer more than anything else.

For some reason I've always had an uncanny feeling about certain places: they've always given me goosebumps. Some particular piece of terrain or even a street corner in Yazoo City brings back in such a rush for me memories of things that have happened on those special spots or things I've been told about. You're that way, too.

DUNLAP: It can be eerie and weird. I've always felt the landscape just pours forth that stuff—the memories, the spirit, the much heralded sense of place. It's a kind of aesthetic archaeology I'm involved in. I've had some interesting things happen to me. My brother and I found an old Navy Colt revolver in a ditch in Webster County when we were growing up. We played with it for years and eventually gave it to a small museum in Holly Springs. We often found arrowheads, too. There were Indian mounds all up and down the Big Black River. And last summer I was digging in my irises in McLean, Virginia, and a minié ball

XII

Dialogue

some Union soldier dropped 125 years ago just came up from the ground there. The same thing can happen with the active imagination. We're living in this realm of imagination. All that information is still under the ground down there. You just have to dig it up and your imagination takes over.

I sense this sort of thing more in this part of the country than anywhere else. I've been in England and visited those prehistoric stone circles and tried to get a feel for what our Druid ancestors were about. It's a little too remote for me. I decline to paint my face blue.

MORRIS: You can't trace the Dunlaps back to the Druids?

DUNLAP: No, but I can to the little village of Dunlop in Scotland. That's far enough. Listen, if I just get them back to Webster County, that's enough, absolutely enough, for me.

MORRIS: You're probably like me: you probably get very much absorbed in déjà vu's. The Disney people were filming this movie of my children's book, *Good Old Boy,* down in Natchez last summer, and the director asked me to come down and talk to the kids. It was exceedingly strange for me.

We are staying in the Sheraton in Natchez. It's about 108 degrees outside and they're out shooting. About six o'clock, six-thirty, I go down to the bar. I'm the only person in the bar. And I'm sitting there on the stool and order an orange juice, Bill.

DUNLAP: Perfectly believable.

MORRIS: And I'm just sitting there thinking about things, and after fifteen or twenty minutes, I feel this tug on my arm. And I look down at this handsome, mischievous looking little boy about eleven. He's got on a blue baseball cap and the clothes of vintage World War II—blue jeans and a short-sleeved cotton shirt that stuck out. And he's got this Southern California accent. "Are you Willie?" I say, "Yeah." "Where've you been, Willie? We've been looking for you for three days." I say, "Who are you?" He says, "I'm Willie." He's playing me—this great little actor.

And over a period of two days it was like ghosts in the sunlight. Here were these Hollywood kids and actors playing my friends from age eleven or so. Here was Maureen O'Sullivan playing my crazy great-aunt, Richard Farnsworth playing my granddaddy, a lady playing my grandma Mamie, and then, my mama and daddy, who were in real life in their thirties. And they started calling me "Son," and I was calling them "Mama" and "Daddy." Watching them film two or three scenes, I thought, My God, this is unreal: I'm looking through a different lens at my own past in flesh and blood. It was a remembrance of a most horrendous kind. Bizarre, but most gratifying.

DUNLAP: I don't even question such occasions anymore. Déjà vu, "charged"—call it what you will—it all goes back to that great "concentration of spirit," as James Dickey would say were he here. People and places can become "charged" just as the icon in religious painting is. The Shroud of Turin is one of my favorites. I once made a painting, loosely based on the Shroud of Turin, called "The King-Sized Sheet of Memphis." It's all about Elvis, the secular saint.

MORRIS: And I've also heard you use the term "hypothetical realism."

DUNLAP: I use it a little tongue-in-cheek because my profession is plagued with so much double-talk—art writing, art

XIV

Dialogue

speak. They've come up with all kinds of realism: there's photo-realism, neo-realism, hyper-realism, anal retentive realism, and any number of other kinds. So "hypothetical realism" is not so farfetched. And at the same time it's very accurate. I work in an objective vein: it isn't real, but it could be. I try to nudge that area below the retina and the cortex of the brain. *Memory* is what I want to jar. I want the viewer to think, "Oh, I know where that is. I've been there. It's Aunt Ruby's place." But, of course, it isn't, because the pictures are invented. I don't make them on site. I make them in the studio. I have to forge them from memory and experience. Hypothetical realism: things that aren't real, but could be.

MORRIS: Is that parallel to—I've used this phrase occasionally, quoting Mark Twain, about writers—"sometimes you've got to lie to tell the truth?" It's invention.

DUNLAP: Yes, Picasso said, "Art is a lie that makes the truth bearable."

MORRIS: I really feel that invention is the highest form of reality.

DUNLAP: There's something that works for me. I remember plowing through that big Joe Blotner biography of Mr. Faulkner, which deals a lot with how he worked, how the stories got made, how this compulsive need to tell a story came about. An idea would lie dormant for a while; then he would hook it together with another one, like a carpenter using whatever is handy, whatever is around.

I've learned to work that way. I draw something and get to know it, and then I move it about. I like to say I have a repertory company of characters and places that I keep shifting to suit my needs. Some of my critics have said, Dunlap's making the same painting over and over. Maybe so, and I'm going to keep on till I get it right. But the paintings are never the same; I couldn't make the same painting twice. It's always going to be about the same thing, though, about jarring memories.

I think you work this way, too. When I was here last fall for that football game, your worktable was so organized. You had those four-by-five cards laid out. It was fascinating for me to see how you did that. It's stream of consciousness, but you know where all those things are and can pull them together. That's so useful to me. Writers have been much more useful to me than painters.

On the way up here, reading your story about your Christmas memory, Linda remarked that it was *her* memory, too. But she didn't grow up in Yazoo City; she grew up in Coral Gables, Florida. And she didn't drive to Jackson, Mississippi; she drove to her grandparent's house on Talavera Street. But there were the same relatives, the same stories, the same sense of things past.

MORRIS: I'd go so far as to conjecture that drawing on memory is the characteristic you and I have most in common. Am I wrong?

DUNLAP: Listen. Your feeling for cemeteries is one I share. When I was looking around for sculpture as a young artist, the only place I could go to find it was in the cemetery. There'd be the occasional third-rate Civil War monument in front of a courthouse somewhere. But here I was in the 1960s in Jackson, Mississippi, and there was no sculpture to be found. That's certainly changed now, but then to find sculpture I'd go to the cemetery, and, not unlike you, as I read in those pieces of yours, I felt buoyed by the cemetery. I felt uplifted by it.

XVI

Dialogue

MORRIS: I know what you mean, Billy. I've just finished a novel called *Taps,* set in a small town during the Korean War. About half of it takes place in cemeteries. Before air conditioning and all the rest, our black nurses would take us to the Yazoo cemetery because it was the coolest place in town. Literally among my earliest memories were the tombstones in the Yazoo City cemetery. I have a little section in *North Toward Home,* a brief, autobiographical coda about playing taps during the Korean War. In my novel I go on from there.

DUNLAP: I once heard taps played as you describe it in *North Toward Home.* I remember, it was in the early fifties at a funeral at one of those red clay country cemeteries in Clarke County. This young boy, home from Korea, had been killed in a car wreck. There he was: he had been shot at in Korea and had come home, only to succumb to drinking and driving fast. I will never forget that sound—someone on a nearby hill playing taps first and then another bugler in the distance playing the echo. It was chilling.

MORRIS: In the cemetery in Raymond they had a ceremony in '87 that tells something about the lead essay in this book, "My Great-Grandfather." It was part of Raymond's sesquicentennial. Hundreds of people were there, and we went out to the cemetery and they unveiled a historical plaque to my great-grandfather. They'd asked me to say a few words and also my son David, as the great-great-grandson. We were sitting at the podium, and all the people in the cemetery were sitting on bales of hay brought out there.

David stood up, and he said, "I'm very honored to be here to help honor my great-great-grandfather, but before I begin, I must make a confession: I'm one-half Yankee." And then he

xvii

Dialogue

went on, made a fine speech, and sat back down. He was sitting next to this old lady, must have been eighty-five years old, who was president of the Hinds County chapter of the United Daughters of the Confederacy. And when good old David sat down, she patted him on the knee and said, "Young man, it's not your fault that you're one-half Yankee."

xviii

Dialogue

DUNLAP: That's yet another burden for you to bear. I've been to that graveyard and to the beautiful battle ground near there. Linda and I were chasing around Champion Hill a couple of years ago. We found the battleground and walked all over it—a very "charged" place.

MORRIS: It's an unusual battleground. I guess they all are, all suffused with terror and sorrow.

DUNLAP: In that essay I liked the part about George Plimpton's great-grandfather.

MORRIS: Plimpton loves the fact that my great-grandfather tried to impeach his great-grandfather, Adelbert P. Ames, who was the Reconstruction governor of Mississippi.

DUNLAP: It seems only right.

MORRIS: I think it's poetic justice. Adelbert Ames lived to be almost a hundred, and Plimpton says when he was a little boy he remembers sitting at his bedside. And here's something else that gave me goosebumps: my friend Bill Styron's great-great-uncle was the state treasurer of Mississippi under my great-great-uncle Henry S. Foote, when he was governor. In fact, they ran in 1851 on a Unionist ticket—a whole slate, from the governor on down. My great-great-uncle ran against Jefferson Davis and beat him by 999 votes. Styron's great-great-uncle was a Mississippian, William Clark—Bill's name is William Clark Styron—and he was a close political associate of my great-great-uncle. Ain't that something? I always like to remind Styron that our two mutual uncles helped preserve the Great Republic, at least for another ten years.

DUNLAP: What happened to those poor courageous moderates in the 1850s? I guess they were overrun by the firebrands. There was no way to keep the Union together.

MORRIS: That war was a tragedy of epic dimensions. As W. B. Yeats suggested, the center did not hold. It's alway hard in extreme times to hold the center. Foote was senior U. S. senator when Jefferson Davis was junior U. S. senator, and they were bitter adversaries. They hated each other. They got in a fist fight once in Washington.

DUNLAP: Politics used to be conducted that way.

MORRIS: You know Mississippi politics has changed when we elect Michael Espy the first black Congressman since Reconstruction. Mike's a Yazoo man, and I'm proud of him.

DUNLAP: It's a curious kind of mix down here. I'm convinced that the African influence made us what we are. We had something else to look at beside ourselves. We would be just like the Midwest if it were not for the black folks' influence There is another William Dunlap from Greenwood, who is as black as he can be and is one of the most sought after bartenders in town. I often see him when I'm there. I went to an arts festival about ten years ago and made several large outdoor billboards. They were placed all around town, and they had "William Dunlap" on them. My bartender buddy said, "Man, I sure appreciate you doing that; it did my reputation a world of good." It's the mix of blacks and whites that gives this state its special quality, I think. When I moved to the mountains of North Carolina, I saw a lot of Anglo-Saxon types like us, but

very few black folks. I said, "Something is not right here. Something's missing. Where are my people?" I felt a little lonely.

MORRIS: A Southerner, a Mississippian, notices very quickly terrains in our own country where there are no black people. I couldn't agree with you more about the intermingling in the Deep South of the Anglo-Saxon and the African. It's always intrigued me—I think it does every Southerner—that deep and complex relationship between the Anglo-Saxon and the African.

DUNLAP: Two people on the run. We define one another and we are interdependent. And we have spread out all over the country, speaking this strange dialect that's a mixture of our English and their African. It's kind of wonderful to bump into Southern black folks in Des Moines, Iowa, and you have much more in common with them than you do with many at the local country club. That's an experience that is universal.

MORRIS: A universal experience: I've run into black cab drivers in New York City from the South and from Mississippi that I actually felt more spiritual kin with than many of the New England WASPs at *Harper's* whom I worked with every day.

DUNLAP: That's well documented, isn't it?

MORRIS: I'll tell you, Bill, one of the most touching things I've seen in the last few years, since I came home, was Richard Wright's daughter Julia coming down here to accept a posthumous award from the University of Mississippi for her father. She'd grown up in Paris and married an African. She'd never been to the South and she was writing a memoir of her father. David Sansing, the history professor at the university, and I took her to Jackson, where she was tracing her father's roots. We found his old school. We found his grandmother's

XX

Dialogue

house that's mentioned in *Black Boy*. She'd not been sure it was still standing, but she had the address on Lynch Street not far from the Jackson State campus. Sansing and I found the house. There it was, but it was now a bar called the Godfather. It was raining, and we had on our raincoats. We went in there, and here were all these black guys playing pool and drinking beer, and they immediately thought that we were homicide detectives. But they were nice, and she saw the house.

Then we took her down to Natchez. David Sansing's son, David Jr., teaches in Natchez, and he'd gotten in touch with the Wright people—her great-aunt, aunts and uncles, cousins. And they met her at their church in Natchez. Sansing and I just took her in; we had the good sense to leave after a while. She was on the verge of tears. *It was her father's family.* Then we went out to this little cemetery in the hills east of Natchez, where her relatives were buried. And then they took us to the little one-room school house where Richard Wright went to school.

DUNLAP: What a saga.

MORRIS: I'd met Wright in Paris, in 1957, and I really liked him. From his writing I'd expected him to be somewhat bellicose, yet he was a warm, friendly, humorous man. We really hit it off—as fellow Mississippians. But it's all that intermingling, the irony of intermingling of the past and present.

DUNLAP: And knowing the same things and having worshipped the same gods, sung the same hymns, eaten the same food, and been abused by the same weather for so long, you've got to have something in common, even if you meet in Paris.

MORRIS: You and I met right here in Oxford. I'd come down for a football weekend in October of '79. Evans Harrington of the Ole Miss English department had asked me to come back here in '80, the following semester, to be writer-in-residence.

DUNLAP: You and young Mr. Shaw came down.

MORRIS: Irwin Shaw's son Adam had never been to the South. So we flew down and rented a car, and we drove through the Delta. I'd not been back to this place in a long, long time, and Adam loved it. We were staying at the Ole Miss Motel. It's not exactly the Waldorf-Astoria but is nonetheless distinctive. He'd been out admiring the girls at the tennis court, and he came back and said, "Morris, you're an absolute fool." I said, "Why?" And he said, "You're from this place, Mississippi, and you don't even have the sense to live here."

DUNLAP: That was a glorious weekend, if you remember. I was about to move to McLean and Dean and Larry Wells, who are my good friends, had asked me to come to the Ole Miss ball game. I'm glad I came.

MORRIS: You were taking a lot of photographs.

DUNLAP: I had that big 300 mm. lens and a sideline pass, and I got the greatest group of photographs you've even seen of fingerprints on cheerleaders' thighs.

MORRIS: But did you look at the ball game? After the thighs?

DUNLAP: I don't even remember who won. It didn't seem to matter.

MORRIS: Georgia: 24 to 21.

DUNLAP: It was just another one of those great gatherings—one of the best parties we've ever had. And it was just good to see everybody—a homecoming.

MORRIS: You and I really need homecomings.

DUNLAP: We do indeed.

xxii

Dialogue

MORRIS: My homecoming on that weekend changed my life. I said, "I'm coming back." I had to be back in January anyway. I went through that semester and couldn't leave.

DUNLAP: You've been in Oxford, then, almost a decade?

MORRIS: It doesn't seem like it.

DUNLAP: Do you think you'll stay?

MORRIS: Oh, yes. I can't live in big cities anymore. I'm a small town boy. Besides, where else can you walk a little way down the street and see Southeastern Conference football, basketball, and baseball? Bill, aren't you envious?

Dialogue

Homecomings

My Great-Grandfather

Detail from *Landscape and Variable: Cedar Ridge—Flight or Fight*

George W. Harper. My great-grandfather: He comes down to me, of course, through the mists of childhood memory. What, after all, is history if not the words handed down through remembrance and kindred blood? I remember his portrait gazing down at me from the wall of my grandmother's house on North Jefferson Street in Jackson, Mississippi: the copious beard, the steel-rimmed glasses, the enigmatic smile. The benign and haunted eyes seemed to beseech the young great-grandson to be wary of the rascals. The relativity of time allows us ineluctable definitions; the years of his life, when passions lay on the land, and vengeance, bloodshed, and retribution, were simultaneously a long time ago, and only yesterday. In Jackson I feel through him the profound pull of my past, and my people's. Jackson was a town he knew very well, its old landmarks and buildings of state. I sense him close at hand.

He had sixteen children, whose births ranged from 1853 to 1878. Four of my great-aunts and uncles were born during the Civil War. My grandmother, whom we called Mamie, was the youngest and the last to die, in 1974 at age ninety-seven. She, naturally, was the one who was the repository of those valiant tales and vanished troubles, who made that old time come alive for me. As I lay drowsily in the next room in that lulled awareness just before sleep, I loved to absorb their voices from the parlor—Mamie's and my great-aunts'—about Mama and Poppa and the Yankees and the long-dead siblings and cousins of Raymond. As they spoke, the big clock on the mantle which he had passed on to them struck each quarter-hour. As I grew up, I believe I felt the palpable challenge, as Jack Burden had in *All the King's Men,* that I must "go out of the house and go into the convulsion of the world, out of history into history and the awful responsibility of time."

My great-grandfather was not, in the strictest sense, a Southern "Bourbon." Although he was well-educated and a gentleman, dignified and extraordinarily brave throughout his seventy years, although his lineage was impeccable—considerably more so than many of the Bourbons who claimed much too much in aristocratic blood—and although his love of Mississippi and the South was deep and abiding, he accepted most of the changes brought about by war and Reconstruction. His complicated devotion to the Union, I surmised, was the skein which held his life together, despite his later bitterness.

His very inheritance was suffused with devotion to the United States of America. His great-grandfather—my great-great-great-great-grandfather—was a legendary, heroic figure: Captain John Harper of Alexandria, Virginia, sea captain and shipping merchant with a fleet of sailing ships docked at the foot of Prince Street in Old Alexandria and called Harper's Wharf. Captain John Harper had twenty-nine children, fortunately by two wives, and there was considerable intermarrying with the Lees and Washingtons and Biddles, perhaps because there were so many of them to go around. He was a dedicated Revolutionist and Federalist, a close friend of Washington, and a frequent guest at the General's Mount Vernon estate.

George W. Harper's grandfather, Captain William Harper of Alexandria, crossed the Delaware with Washington in December, 1776, in Captain Robb's Company, Colonel Stewart's Thirteenth Pennsylvania Regiment. He fought in the battles of Trenton, Princeton, Brandywine, and Germantown, and was one of Washington's wintertime lieutenants at Valley Forge. My cousin Frank O'Beirne, in his history of the Harpers of Virginia and Mississippi, wrote that on September 18, 1793, Captain William Harper, with his artillery company, went with General Washington to Washington, D.C., to lay the cornerstone of the United States Capitol. His artillery fired a salute as part of the ceremony, and he returned to his country home after that with Washington for what was described as a "most sumptuous dinner."

Captain William's artillery company of the Alexandria Blues fired the minute guns at Washington's interment at Mount Vernon. George W. Harper's mother, Sarah Keyes Harper, was the daughter of George North, another captain of the Revolution. All of them are buried in the old Presbyterian cemetery in Alexandria.

I do not cite this to titillate the DAR, but to emphasize my great-grandfather's intense American legacies. During the debate on the Compromise of 1850, he would write of "the great Conservative Republican principles which were planted in our heart in childhood in Virginia, and have never ceased to strengthen with our strength and grow with our growth. Fanaticism and folly—ultraism and sectionalism . . . are dogmas at which every patriot breast must stand appalled."

In the times I have dwelled in Virginia, I myself have often felt what must have been its great contrast with the raw, unsettled Mississippi frontier to which my great-grandfather departed in 1844. It must not have been easy to leave the Old Dominion for Mississippi, but there were many such departures in that day, and the linkage between the two states was a direct one; Virginia, the Father of Presidents, was the uncle of us all.

When, in the 1930s, my spinster great-aunt Susie retired from her job at the Coca-Cola Bottling Plant in Raymond—I was told she put the caps on the bottles—she had saved her money to take the bus to Harper's Ferry, West Virginia. When she arrived, she searched the telephone book and found a Harper. She went to the address and knocked on the door. After a long wait she heard a window opening upstairs, and a gruff query: "What do you want?" "I'm a Harper!" Aunt Susie said. "So what?" the voice shouted. "So am I!" and the window banged down.

George W. Harper was born in Alexandria in 1824. As a child he moved with his parents to Wheeling, then in Virginia. He started learning the newspaper business at age thirteen on the Wheeling *Daily Gazette*. "There's ink in your blood," my grandmother Mamie once said of him and me, as I was leaving for college. In Wheeling he frequently saw and heard Henry Clay, who became his ideal as patriot and statesman. He could have done worse. From those early years he developed his strong Whig stance. During the "coonskin, hard cider, log cabin, and red paper" canvass of 1840 he edited a campaign periodical, at age sixteen, for Harrison and Tyler. At eighteen he and a partner bought the Wheeling *Daily Gazette* and he was for a brief time its editor.

In 1844, at age twenty-one, he took a river steamer to Vicksburg, then travelled overland to Raymond, a graceful and languid old town near Jackson, a twin county seat of Hinds County. He was migrating to Mississippi in that decade in which black slaves were outnumbering whites in the total population of the state, with all which that entailed, tie inhuman labor of the Delta, the splitting of families.

In Raymond he went to work on the *Southwestern Farmer*, a newspaper owned by his uncle Green North, who had earlier emigrated from Virginia. On the ruins of that paper he and a partner established the Raymond *Gazette*. In 1848 he was a delegate to the convention that nominated Zachary Taylor for president. The name of the paper was later changed to the *Hinds County Gazette*; it bears that name today. He subsequently became the sole owner and editor-in-chief.

The *Gazette* developed a reputation of fearlessness and honesty, a guardian of public interests, one of the finest journals in the South of that era, moderate and civilized in the white conservative context. He was sometimes referred to as the "Chevalier Bayard" of the Mississippi press. He was chosen mayor of Raymond and major of the local militia. In 1851, and again in 1853, he was elected to the state House of Representatives from Hinds County on the Union Party ticket.

Major Harper, in 1852, married my great-grandmother, Anna Sims, of Clinton and Port Gibson. She was the niece of General Cowles Mead, distinguished in the history of Mississippi as a territory—as territorial governor and founding colonel of the First Mississippi Infantry, which Jefferson Davis later commanded as the Mississippi Rifles in the Mexican War. General Mead arrested Aaron Burr near Natchez in his strange odyssey of treason. My great-aunt, Ella Mead Harper, born in 1873, was named after General Mead.

My great-grandmother was likewise related to Henry S. Foote, who as United States senator had delivered the dedicatory address for the Washington Monument, had cooperated with Clay on the compromise measures of 1850, and had defeated Jefferson Davis for governor of Mississippi in 1851. (The writer William Styron's great-uncle William Clark was a close ally of Foote, and was elected state treasurer on the same ticket.) Foote called my great-grandmother "my favorite niece" and introduced her to my great-grandfather for the first time in the Governor's Mansion. The Grand Old Union was in the family.

By all accounts, Major Harper grew to be regarded as one of the most prominent and respected men of his time in Mississippi, a man of integrity and one of the South's best editors, noted not only for his vivid prose but, in the tradition of the day, as an effective speaker as well.

This is what they would write about him in his newspaper on his death in 1894. I remember reading the florid words as a child:

> When grim-visaged war burst in all its tremendous fury upon the fair southland, the gallant major entered the confederate service and was actively engaged in the Quartermaster department until the close of the struggle; an affliction of the eyes which he had suffered from youth rendered him unfit for fighting in the ranks. After grim visaged war had smoothed his wrinkled front, Major Harper returned to the Gazette office, allied himself with the Democratic Party, which had absorbed the old Whig organi-

zation, and through the dread days of reconstruction, when the furies of peace were worse than the terrors of war, he advocated conciliatory measures and a peaceful acceptance of the terms of surrender. . . .

He did indeed fight hard against secession, but as with the Lees and the countless others, finally went with his native South. From my reading of his life, as expressed in his editorials, and from what was handed down to me by my family, he sensed that the dissolution would bring about the bloodiest war in the history of the human race, and he was right. The statistics of death, mutilation, and disease, in a total population on both sides of no more than twenty-eight million, were astounding, more than one million young men. In that war, seventy-eight thousand men of Mississippi fought in the Confederate Army. More than fifty-nine thousand were wounded, and over half of those died. Little wonder that my Harper great-aunts never married. Not until the carnage of the Western Front in World War One would organized blood-letting compare with our Civil War. In this perspective, the vigorous efforts of men like my great-grandfather to preserve the Union against all odds—the irony and sorrow of it all—elicit my sympathy. It is not surprising that these horrific casualties, largely incurred on home ground, which obliterated the potential white leaders of the South—a generation literally gone with the wind—incurred such pain and rancor in such essentially moderate Southerners as my great-grandfather.

In 1866 the state of Mississippi allotted one-fifth of its revenues for the purchase of artificial limbs for its returning veterans. Shelby Foote, our American Homer, cited what he called "the butcher's bill" for the nation, and quoted Anaximander from 2,500 years ago. "It is necessary that things should pass away into that from which they are born. For things must pay one another the penalty and compensation for their injustice according to the ordinance of time." So it was, Foote surmised, with the Confederacy, and "so will it be one day for the other nations of earth, if not for earth itself." Arnold Toynbee wrote that, to most people, history was something that happened to someone else a long time ago. "But if I had been a boy in the American South in the 1870s," he said, "my parents would have told me that history happened to us." In one editorial after another after that war, my great-grandfather's animus against the diehard white Southern secessionists seemed even more intractable than against the Northern radicals.

With forty-three years of his editorials in the *Hinds County Gazette* available, I could choose many byroads. But I wish to concentrate briefly here on his consistent position throughout his life as a Unionist. Though he upheld slavery, and was in many ways a creature of his day—aren't indeed we all?—before the tragic breakdown from 1861 to 1865 and then again after it, he unwaveringly chose the Union of the States over any other arrangement Americans could devise for themselves, the only bulwark against chaos on our disparate, unformed continent.

As an editor and public leader, he lived and wrote during the complicated time of the 1850s, when the collapse of the great republic seemed always at hand. He lived through military defeat, economic ruin, and social revolution. In the confusion and destruction following the war, he seldom allowed his bitterness as an aristocratic white against what he considered to be the extreme elements in the North to deter him from that Unionist vision. Surely he was an ironic man, and an intellectual. He cared for the newly-freed black man, within the limits of his time, and he comprehended something of the nuance and complexity of the black in his state better than almost all of his conservative white contemporaries. He never failed to castigate those he deemed turncoat Southerners and especially Northern radicals whom he thought desired a scorched-earth policy. Yet his recurring animosity, voiced time and again in his post-war editorials, against those who would destroy the South of his memory, was always assuaged by his emotional ties to the larger America.

Professor Thomas B. Alexander, in an article in the April, 1961, number of the *Journal of Mississippi History,* cited Major Harper during the post-war period as a surpassing example of old-line Whiggery in the South:

> His devotion to Whig Party principles and to Henry Clay as the personification of Whiggery, as well as his continuing distrust of the Democratic Party, reflects the attitude of many old-line Southern Whigs. Unlike such former Whigs as James L. Alcorn, Harper never co-operated politically with Mississippi Republicans after the war except in fusion party campaigns in which the Mississippi Democratic and Conservative Parties supported a moderate Republican against a radical Republican.

The National Whig Party had begun to disintegrate in the early 1850s. In Mississippi the Whigs were resoundingly defeated all through the fifties. As early as December, 1851, Major Harper counselled "prudence, patience, and patriotism" on the compromise issues of the previous year. He was dismayed by the Democratic Party, which had been "secessionized and abolitionized." All through the 1850s he assailed "the Monster of Secession, and its multitude of poisons." Yet, as a loyal Southerner, he would write: "The South is united to a man, without distinction as a party, in firm and unyielding opposition to the demands and aggressions of Northern fanaticism . . . We have been, and still are, 'one and indivisible' in everything that relates to the protection of Southern rights and institutions." He appealed for moderation to "every real friend of the peace and quiet, prosperity and glory, of our Union of States."

From my grandmother Mamie I learned that he owned one slave, a domestic named James who worked in the house and the newspaper shop and who stayed with the family until his death in the 1880s—deeply loved, Mamie said, by the Harper children. "We believe that our institutions are in themselves just and provident," Major Harper had written in 1856, "that they insure on a whole people who are industrious, social, and well-affected; and that they secure us against the evils of pauperism, thievery, and outlawry."

In 1860 he supported John Bell for President on the Union Party ticket. When war came he continued his role as major in the militia and published the *Gazette* until May 12 of 1863. On that day the Federal troops occupied Raymond, after a fierce battle attendant to the march on Jackson and before the final siege of Vicksburg. A Federal captain under orders from General Grant supervised the destruction of Harper's printing presses; they were deposited in the town well. My great-grandmother helped nurse the wounded of both sides in the family house. She took down a letter, my grandmother Mamie would tell me years later, from a dying twenty-year old soldier from Illinois to his mother, and made sure the Federal officers sent it up through the lines. The house, I was told, ran with blood, which dripped down the rain gulleys. As I was reminded over and over as a boy, the family cow soon disappeared. My great-grandmother, with several mouths to feed, went to the captain of the Federal troops and complained that his soldiers had stolen their cow. "Find this lady a cow," the captain ordered his staff, and then graciously escorted her home. "Mama said he was such a nice man," Mamie and my great-aunts would say to me as late as the 1940s sitting in the parlor on North Jefferson in Jackson, "such a nice honest man who cared," but when the original cow wandered home the next day, and the herd increased to two, Yankee chivalry was not rewarded with the return of the merchandise.

The *Gazette* resumed publication on October 7, 1865. My great-grandfather declared in a maiden editorial that new materials had been purchased and an office fitted up opposite the courthouse. He pledged that the paper would continue to be "a fair and truthful and eminently conservative, practical and useful county newspaper, pledged only to liberty and law, and opposing all dangerous experiments and unprofitable strifes. Having opposed secession and disunion vigorously, both with his pen and vote, but did his whole duty to the native section when an armed force came from the frozen north devastating and destroying our beautiful state, the undersigned asks, in his more mature age, what was so generously afforded him in his youth—a large circulation for his paper, and an advertising patronage commensurate with the business of the country."

Having never tolerated the secessionist Democrats before the War, he now allied with them, although he still retained his quintessential Whig philosophy. This was evident in many of his conciliatory editorials from 1865 to 1878. While he advocated acceptance of defeat and the terms of surrender, he consistently expressed his antipathy toward Northern abolitionists, as evidenced in an editorial of January, 1866, concerning the reuniting of Northern and Southern churches. In the North "the pulpits are filled with bloody men," and this especially applied to New Englanders.

In October, 1865, he had written: "As things look at present, we don't know but that we shall all have to become Democrats if we presume, hereafter, to take any part in National politics. But there can never again be a Democratic organization in the Southern states with the old party leaders and their practices, theories and platforms."

There was, of course, no Marshall Plan after that war. The land was desolated and impoverished and whites and blacks dubious of their future when he wrote of the National Thanksgiving, which the Washington authorities were setting aside to honor good feelings and the restored Union. It was a bleak and despairing piece. A land of plenty "has been swept with the sword, the torch, and by the robber, and now lies despoiled, devastated . . . an unwilling victim to Northern brute force. . . ."

In June, 1866, he cited the coming of the Fourth of July, once a joyous occasion, now one that would bring sorrow. After all, Vicksburg, only thirty miles to the west, had capitulated on July 4, 1863. "We regret that . . . our veneration for that day," he wrote, "has passed away. Some of the most joyful scenes of our youth cluster around such occasions. We would have it so again. . . ."

Yet the grandson of Captain William Harper and advocate

of the Union had hope. "But we do not utterly despair of the Union . . . Someday the people of the South, always magnanimous, will unite with patriots in every section of the Union, and the Stars and Stripes will again be held aloft, the Constitution venerated, the laws vindicated."

During the Presidential Reconstruction of 1865 to 1867, Andrew Johnson's lenient plan was wholeheartedly supported by Major Harper. He continued his pro-Union editorials. In June, 1866, he proposed a national convention of "the friends of President Johnson's policy" without regard to former political affinities. "There are conservative Republicans at the north, Whigs at the south—supporters of Bell, of Douglas, of Breckenridge, in 1861, in all parts of the Union, who would enroll under such a banner."

His striking piece in the *Gazette* of May 3, 1867, symbolized the short-lived racial harmony of that moment. It has curious modern resonances. A meeting of the citizens of Lowndes County had just been held in the courthouse in Columbus. "The white man and the black man met together to talk over the mighty events of the living present," he wrote, "and carve out a line of conduct for the future that will give to our section repose and comfort. The most prominent citizens of the country were present to talk over the issues of the day with their former slaves. Blacks and whites delivered addresses, and committees were formed to confer with the freedmen to secure harmony of action." He reported that a Conservative Union Party was established to affirm that the Federal Government was supreme, "that politically the white and black man of the South occupy the same position under the laws ... and recognizing all citizens as entitled to the same political rights, recommending the establishment of schools for all classes, pledging the freemen our warmest sympathies and aid, guaranteeing him the enjoyment of the rights of person and property, and inviting all men, without distinction of race, color, or servitude, to connect themselves with the party."

Then came the recalcitrance of the state legislature, the enactment of the Black Codes and the blatant rejection of the Constitution of 1868. Mississippi would be the next-to-the-last state, before Georgia, to be re-admitted to the Union, in 1870. With the stringent Congressional Reconstruction, which lasted from 1867 to 1875, Major Harper was resigning himself to the beleaguered state of affairs in Mississippi and the South. With the military government and the disfranchisement of many whites, he editorialized in June, 1867: "The South is a conquered country. At the moment we are at the mercy of the Northern radical thieves and robbers. We cannot help ourselves—we must submit to their requirements be they ever so unmerciful, unjust, and infamous." He was a delegate to the state Democratic Convention in Jackson in early 1868 and praised its resolution which "fully sanctions the principles and policy of the National Democratic Party, in their efforts by constitutional and peaceful means to overthrow Radicalism and re-establish the Union of the States. . . ."

Yet even with his new Democratic Party allegiance, he never forgot his old Whig affinities and seldom disassociated the Democrats from secession and its results. "Treason and disunion prevailed," he wrote in a post-war editorial against the Democrats of Mississippi. "The tree bore its legitimate fruits. Rebellion inaugurated hell on earth."

The lines were so tightly drawn, he declared, between the Radicals and the Democrats, that the Old Whigs must reluctantly vote with the latter. In late 1868 he called upon the principles of "the old and reliable Union sentiment of Mississippi . . . the men who hung out faithful and true to the end, and voted against Secession and Secessionists at the state convention held just after the first election of Mr. Lincoln . . . to send a live committee to Washington to represent the true sentiment of the true and permanent Union people of Mississippi."

As the extremes were being drawn in the state, there remained a steady theme in his editorials from 1869 to 1875, the old Unionist Whig imploring the necessity of harmony and unity, nostalgic almost in its unfolding. "The Whigs," he wrote, ". . . were opposed to Secession and War, and devoted to the Union of the States." These men, he continued, and there were large numbers of them, were still intensely loyal. They "are the proper men to carry Mississippi back into the sisterhood of states. And we believe the leaders of the two extreme Parties of the State—the carpetbaggers and the Ultra-Democrats—now begin to look this fact full in the face."

In mid-1869 he despaired: "The National Government, heavily armed, has us, who are unarmed and naked, by the throat, with a bayonet just entering the skin of the left breast. The Goverment tells us to do so and so, and if we don't do it, it will do it for us! . . . Mississippi will ultimately be reconstructed on just the terms, and no other, dictated at Washington, and dictated by General Ames from his easy chair in Jackson."

Before James L. Alcorn took the lead in supporting the congressional plan of Reconstruction, my great-grandfather wrote a number of editorials in his favor. Reminding his readers that he had not endorsed Alcorn as the Republican candidate in the gubernatorial election of 1869, he wrote: "In old times General Alcorn was a zealous and unflinching Whig—a Union Whig—an 'old-line Whig.' We served in the Mississippi legislature with him in 1852, and again in 1854, and we can now certify that he was ever true . . . to Mississippi, true to the best interests of her people, and true to the Union of States. We believe General Alcorn will prove equal to the present emergency." A few weeks later, in 1870, he described Alcorn as "an old personal and political friend" who was just stepping into power. "We wish to call his mind back to old and halcyon days and remove some of the rough and unpleasant thoughts engendered by a desperate contest. We want Alcorn to recognize that although he had been opposed by almost the entire white element in the state, there were still white men among us, his friends of former years, who would stand by him if his policy would permit them to do so—if he would hold out the 'olive branch' instead of the negro with a pistol in one hand and a torch in the other."

In June, 1871, Major Harper published his own political platform, which included "the protection of all, whites and blacks, in the quiet enjoyment of their civil and political rights" and "acquiescence in the Constitutional Amendments"—the thirteenth, fourteenth and fifteenth national amendments enfranchising the black man and upholding his full civil rights. His support of the constitutional amendments, he admitted, did not accord with his past views. "We now for the first time acquiesce completely in them. We are led to this course, not through choice, but . . . by the stern logic of events." From whatever rationale, it was, to say the least, unusual for a white Mississippi conservative in 1871 to uphold the sweeping new amendments.

In the turbulent 1870s his words often assumed an uncharacteristically strident tone, expressive of his growing disenchantment with the state government under the Radical Republicans. Citing the large increases in property taxes and the dispossession of many whites, he wrote: "We seek to overthrow the party whose men and schemes have entailed all this evil upon an impoverished and oppressed people. The plunderers must be driven out or the honest people must emigrate. Which shall it be? 'Under which King, Benzonian, live or die?'"

General Adelbert P. Ames, the military governor of Mississippi before his appointment to the U.S. Senate, had been elected governor in 1873. Perhaps there is irony that Adelbert P. Ames was the great-grandfather of my close friend and collaborator in New York, the writer George Plimpton, and that my great-grandfather became, in those formidable times, Plimpton's great-grandfather's most persistent and vituperative foe. In late 1874, Harper threw down the gauntlet before Ames. "The *Hinds County Gazette*, through all four long and dreary years of Radical rule in Mississippi, while at all times decidedly anti-Radical, has ever been mild, moderate, and conservative . . . We are now satisfied, however, that nothing has been, or can be gained by moderation and kindness—in fact, we now think, that moderation and kindness have rather invited new outrages and encouraged the official thieves and rascals to additional atrocities . . . We must 'fight the devil with fire.' The *Hinds County Gazette* proposes to make it lively for Governor Ames and his thieves during the year 1875."

In that tempestuous year, as if an all-consuming war had never been fought, Mississippi seemed on the brink of wholesale violence. Race riots erupted throughout the state. When Governor Ames disbanded the state militia, Democrats devised their plan of fraudulence and intimidation which led to widespread success at the polls. The Democrats won a two-thirds majority in the state Senate and a majority in the House which led, of course, to the impeachment proceedings against several Republican officials, including Ames. My great-grandfather was again elected to the legislature in that year on the Democratic ticket. I have inherited from my grandmother a composite portrait of the Mississippi House, George W. Harper surrounded by black faces. When, in 1876, it became apparent that Ames could not survive an impeachment vote and he submitted his resignation, Harper voted yea with the majority dismissing the articles against him.

In an editorial of July, 1876, he finally pronounced: "By an effort without parallel in the annals of our political history, the Radical thieves have been overthrown and dispersed in Hinds County and the state of Mississippi . . ." And in November, 1878, he wrote retrospectively: "Ever since the war . . . Mississippi has dangled at the tail of Northern political organizations . . . We have voted and acted as they have directed, not presuming to ask questions, or to doubt the right of our Northern friends to dictate a policy . . . The Republican Party," he concluded, "is as dead as Hector, not only in Mississippi, but in the South and the Union . . . It is, thank heaven, beyond doing harm, and now is the time for the inauguration of a Mississippi Policy, and a

Mississippi Party, independent of dictation from any quarter, yet loyal wholly to the prosperity of the Union."

A number of prominent Democrats, my grandmother and great-aunts later would tell me, had asked him to stand for governor in those latter years, but he refused. He said he was worn out. He retired from the *Gazette* in 1883. His son Samuel Dawson Harper, who like his father had gone into newspapering in his teens, succeeded him as editor.

My great-grandfather died in Raymond in 1894. My great-grandmother Anna Sims Harper left Raymond and lived in Jackson until her death in 1912 in an old house on Griffith Street behind the Hotel Robert E. Lee. I was always told that she was a gentle yet intrepid Southern woman, much like Mrs. Maud Faulkner, of Oxford, mother of a writer, indomitable and true—she had lived first-hand through the blood and trauma and retained her sanity and humor toward life, shepherding her brood of children through war and Reconstruction into what-ever passed as peace; whose children mattered first to her, as my grandmother told me, yet who cared for the black freedmen and women of Raymond as if they were her own too—as if they had lived mutually and together through that great catastrophic magnitude of events.

The Harpers' antebellum house where my mother and grand-mother were born is still there in Raymond, restored now by others—the present mayor of Raymond and his family—to the grace and eminence it lost in those years of impoverishment and dispossession. They are all buried in the Harper plot in the old part of the Raymond cemetery. Fifty yards or so from the family plot is an enclosure of graves—the dozens of

Confederate soldiers killed in the Battle of Raymond, watered and manicured still by the ladies of the town. Just before my beloved grandmother Mamie died in Yazoo City in 1974, she said: "Put me down next to Percy, and to Momma and Pappa, and say goodbye and close the gate behind you." A historical plaque to Major Harper was unveiled in ceremonies there in 1987.

And today . . . and today? The things I might tell my great-grandfather: about the civil rights movement of the 1960s, or the massive integration of the schools in 1970, or the ten young black men who were the starting teams for Ole Miss and Mississippi State in a recent basketball game, or the Metrocenter shopping mall in Jackson, or national homogeneity in a television culture, or that Mississippi may be the only place that really cares about integration anymore, or that the party of Generals Ulysses S. Grant and William Tecumseh Sherman and Adelbert P. Ames has managed to come back again to Mississippi—and apparently in much more substantial force than before. But none of this would be fair, for those were his own days, and they were impassioned ones. In a speech to old Northern veterans in 1884, nearly twenty years after Appomattox, Oliver Wendell Holmes said: "I think that, as life is action and passion, it is required of a man that he should share the passion and action of his time, at peril of being judged not to have lived at all."

And, withal, I believe my great-grandfather would be gratified and bemused to know that his great-great-grandson David Rae Morris, having grown up in New York City and attended college in New England, was living and working as a talented photographer in Mississippi, searching the old, tragic landscapes for his material. Major Harper had bequeathed something of his legacy to myself also, his great-grandson. For my great-grandfather was, after all, a writer.

25

My Great-Grandfather

Anybody's
Children

But above all the courthouse; the center, the focus, the hub; sitting looming in the center of the county's circumference like a single cloud in its ring of horizon, laying its vast shadow to the uttermost rim of horizon; musing, brooding, symbolic, and ponderable, tall as cloud, solid as rock, dominating all: protector of the weak, judicate and curb of the passions and lusts, repository and guardian of the aspirations and the hopes. . . .

William Faulkner
Requiem for a Nun

ee Goodwin and Nancy Manigo were tried and convicted of murder here, and Mink Snopes was dispatched from here to the infamous Parchman for killing Jack Houston, everyone having neglected that Jack Houston deserved killing. It is a muted, high-ceilinged old courtroom with ornate chandeliers and long oaken pews for seats and two graceful outside balconies with stately white columns on the north and south ends, the latter with an unencumbered view of the Confederate soldier below gazing down South Lamar. As in the old honored movies, the empty spaces around the bench, the jury box, and the counsels' tables allow the lawyers to peregrinate freely as they question the witnesses. It was every courtroom of our small-town Southern childhoods, a *To Kill A Mockingbird* milieu, where we would surreptitiously tip-toe into the galleries, barefoot sometimes in the summers, and absorb awe-struck and a little frightened the imperishable litanies of rapine, deceit, and death, the stark, brooding secrets of the adult cosmos. "A scary room to be tried in for your life," a law professor from Ole Miss whispered to me during one particularly significant cross-examination, and I knew what he meant.

"The murder of the century in this town," an habitué of the courthouse called it, and it was a trial which resonated with

Old Testament pain and retribution, and with money and grief, horror and fear, and startling déjà vu's from the Faulknerian corpus.

It was May, slightly more than one year since the crime, and the magnolias on the courthouse greenswards were in early blossom, and from the lawns was the clean sweet smell of newly-cut grass. The defendant was a twenty-two-year-old Ole Miss student named Doug Hodgkin, son of a prominent bank president from Winchester, Kentucky—an SAE, a business major, scion of big inherited wealth. The victim was a beautiful Ole Miss graduate student named Jeanie Gillies, age twenty-four, daughter of a widely respected doctor from Magnolia, Mississippi, honor graduate of Belhaven College who had taught second grade for a time in Jackson. Defendant and victim had known each other for five weeks. The autopsy report had shown that she was six to eight weeks pregnant.

The defendant was on trial for capital murder. After the crime he had served three months in the county jail, then was released on $250,000 bond, the largest in the history of the county. At about 10:00 A.M. on May 2, 1986, the victim had been found nude in her apartment at 602 South Lamar, severely beaten about the head by a blunt object, viciously sodomized, and strangled. She was bound with her hands behind her and gagged and was lying face down in the bathroom of her apartment. Her body was smeared with her own feces. The chief medical examiner of Mississippi called it one of the two or three most brutal sexual assaults he had ever investigated.

The defendant, represented by a battery of eloquent, respected, highly-skilled Mississippi lawyers with voluminous files and the counsel of expert consultants, was pleading innocent. Among

Deer Head for Infinity, 1983
Oil and graphite on paper; 70¼″ × 52¼″
Courtesy of Sherry French Gallery, New York, New York
Photo by Walter Smalling

Ridge Run—Fresh Flowers, 1988
Oil and dry pigment on paper; 75″ × 50″
Courtesy of the artist
Photo by Jack Meyer

*Landscape and Variable: Antietam
Cut—Deep Iris Watch*, 1988

Painted construction: polymer paint, linen,
  wood, deer hide, shells, 30″ × 160″ × 11″
Courtesy of Sherry French Gallery, New York,
  New York
Photo by Jack Kotz

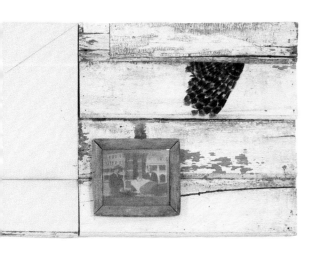

*Landscape and Variable: Cedar
Ridge—Flight or Fight*, 1988

Painted construction: polymer paint, linen,
  wood, bird wing; 30″ × 128½″ × 6″
Courtesy of Sherry French Gallery, New York,
  New York
Photo by Jack Kotz

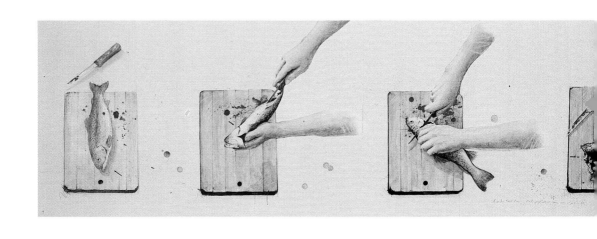

Rainbow Trout Farm, 1978
Oil and dry pigment on paper; 24″ ×
  118″ diptych
Courtesy of the artist
Photo by Jack Meyer

*Landscape and Variable: Deer Hide—
Willow Seek*, 1987

Painted construction: polymer paint, canvas,
  wood, steel, deer hide, willow ball; 30″ ×
  132″ × 7″
Courtesy of Sherry French Gallery, New York,
  New York

Meditations on the Origins of Agriculture in America, 1987

Painted construction: wood, canvas, polymer
and oil paint, paper, steel, snake skin; 48"
  × 96" × 24"
Courtesy of Sherry French Gallery, New York,
  New York
Photo by Jack Meyer

Landscape and Variable: Indian Paint Brush, 1987
Polymer paint on canvas; 94″ × 68″
Courtesy of U. S. State Department, Art in Embassies Program
Photo by Jack Meyer

Rose Red Roof Rot Run, 1989
Painted construction: polymer paint, wood metal, ice pick, fresh flowers
    and art supplies; 63″ × 31½″ × 12″
Courtesy of Sherry French Gallery, New York, New York
Photo by Adam Reich

Landscape and Variable: The Bounty and Burden of History, 1988
Mixed media and polymer paint on canvas; 66″ × 94″
Courtesy of Sherry French Gallery, New York, New York
Photo by Adam Reich

Aqua Garden—Fish and Flowers, 1988
Oil and dry pigment on paper; 86" × 60"
Courtesy of the artist
Photo by Jack Meyer

Three Deer Head for Antietam, 1982
Oil and dry pigment on paper; 47½″ × 93½″
Courtesy of Mr. and Mrs. Meredith Long, Houston, Texas

the inexhaustible fount of rumors was that their legal fees would reach half a million dollars. There were no eyewitnesses and no confession. The time of death that May 2 had been established at approximately 2:00 A.M. The defendant himself had telephoned the ambulance service at about 10:00 A.M. He and Miss Gillies had been together at a party on the campus the night before, and at a bar on the square where the Tangents were playing. They were last seen at 1:00 A.M. by one "Pizza Bob," a colorful local entrepreneur well-known to Ole Miss students for more than twenty years, at his establishment on University Avenue. In testimony Pizza Bob would describe Hodgkin as drunk, but "not all that drunk."

They returned to her apartment. It was Hodgkin's claim that he shortly left Miss Gillies in the living room and retired to a small bedroom area adjacent to the living room about eight feet from where she was soon to be beaten on the head and gagged. He went soundly to sleep and did not awaken until around 9:30 A.M. He discovered the body in the bathroom and summoned the ambulance. He told the ambulance driver and later the police: "I think she committed suicide."

Shortly after 10:00 A.M. on that day, Dean Faulkner Wells, niece of William Faulkner, was sweeping the walkway to her house, where she lives with her husband Larry, owner of the Yoknapatawpha Press. It had been the house of her grand-mother Maud Faulkner, Faulkner's mother. Faulkner and Miss Maud would sit often on the front gallery watching the cars go by. He wrote a portion of *Absalom! Absalom!* on a table in the dining room. The street which runs by the house, Lamar Boulevard, is the grand thoroughfare of the town, lined with gracious old homes of an earlier day, with broad porches and swings half-hidden by flourishing magnolias and hickories and sumacs and pines and oaks and gums. This auspicious boulevard intersects the courthouse and goes around it to resume as North Lamar.

As Dean swept the sidewalk, Miss Durley Roach, an elderly Oxford lady who lives in the neighborhood, walked by. Dean remembered her from her childhood as the ticket-seller at the Ritz Theater, where she and her uncle would go to Charlie Chan movies.

"Deanie," Miss Durley said, "there's a corpse in that house!" It turned out that Miss Durley owned a police scanner and had just heard an exchange between the ambulance driver and the police station. Their vehicles were almost immediately on the scene.

The murder house was two doors down and mere yards from the Faulkner house. A small brick duplex usually rented by Ole Miss students stood between the two domiciles. Not too long before, two outstanding black Ole Miss Rebel football players, Buford McGee and Andre Townsend, lived in the brick duplex. On the afternoon Buford and Andre were drafted by the San Diego Chargers and Denver Broncos, I well remember, several Ole Miss coeds festooned the little house with red-and-blue balloons and put up a huge sign: *"Buford and Andre. NFL Bound."* Several of us brought them some Andre Champagne and celebrated. The party spilled outside onto the lawn of what was to be the murder house.

Miss Gillies was murdered in the back apartment of 602 South Lamar. (William Faulkner's grandparents had once lived in a substantial old house on the exact site, later moved intact up the block.) A graduate student lived in another apartment upstairs and had been awake all night studying for exams. Other students lived in Buford and Andre's former place, no more than twenty yards or so from the crime. Immediately on the south side, only yards away, was another house divided into apartments, where Ole Miss students also lived.

At dusk that day I found the students who rented these houses mingling trance-like near the premises. On South Lamar an un-broken string of cars moved slowly by, each pausing briefly in front of the house. The murder apartment had been sealed—great strips of heavy tape on the door and windows. The students were stunned and subdued. None had heard anything in the early morning hours. Dean Faulkner Wells had heard the chimes from the courthouse two blocks away—otherwise nothing. Even her two little dogs did not bark. This dark, eerie neighborhood silence added to the mystery and to the boundless rumors which became epic as the months unfolded.

My merchant friends around the square reported that busi-ness was down thirty percent during the trial. I saw no reason to disbelieve them. The courtroom was so crowded, with peo-ple standing two-deep along the walls, that the jury—eight women, four men, including one black man—complained at one point of being distracted. More than a few of the spec-tators, often widows, seemed embarrassed by their own un-swerving presence and sat unobtrusively in corners. Domes-tic arguments of an arcane nature erupted. Husbands criticized their wives for being away from home all day for a week and a half and returning to talk of nothing but blood, semen, and feces, and the dimensions of the murder apartment, the wine bottle with the fingerprints allegedly wiped off, the unlocked back door, the cold demeanor of the defendant, and protean points of law. That inevitable cadre of courthouse square people who will sit diligently through auto collision, alimony, and petty larceny cases—they are archetypal to this day in any Southern town—were there from dawn to dusk. Silas Gault, the former nightwatchman at the Ole Miss experimental marijuana field, and Motee Daniel, Faulkner's old bootlegger, were surrounded during the recesses by the quizzical seeking information on legal procedure and on the likely mood of the jury. Others wanted the predictions of these intense boulevardiers. "Guilty," Silas said, "I don't miss many." Motee observed: "I know one of the jury fellows. He'll be locked up ten days. He'll sway either way for a pint of vodka." In the gallery during one recess, I overheard several children—boys and girls who could not have been older than the fifth grade—openly talking about homosexuality, rape, sodomy, drugs, and the age of the fetus, a conversation which would have been somewhat inconceivable in the fifth grade of Yazoo City, Mississippi, forty years ago. Numerous young people were there every day. "I can identify with him," a luminous, beautiful Ole Miss coed said to me. "I've been partying a lot. I've been passed out like that before. It's easy to see yourself in that situation. It's scary." During the lunch recesses many of the observers sat on the benches outside and dined on sandwiches and hot dogs ordered from the Jitney Jungle next to the jailhouse up the way. As one such group enjoyed this provender, a man in overalls driving a pickup truck slowed down near their bench and shouted: "This looks like the sunporch at Whitfield!"*[1] At a small birthday

---

[1]*In Mississippi "Whitfield" is generic from one's very childhood. It is the state mental hospital.

dinner one evening I noted the celebrants graphically discussing the autopsy photographs without pause in their eating. "I can't take this anymore," a businessman who had attended every session finally said in the gallery toward the denouement. "I'm going back to the office to sell *insurance.*"

What, in the human provenance, was the source of this horrific and infectious obsession? Everyone asked this of himself. It was the old hypnotic spell cast upon all of us by mayhem and suffering—the incandescent voyeurism of the imperfect human heart. It was the contemplation in the most undiluted communal Southern-American locale of our own secret guilts and fears, of the flawed equities and prescriptions which are somehow the best man had devised for himself in his governance in the medieval mists through time. It was these things and more.

"Lord, he looks just like everyone else, doesn't he?" someone whispered of the alleged murderer—a tall, slender, handsome young man of dark countenance, impeccable in a grey suit, dress shirt, and tie. Many women in the audience, old and young, were physically drawn to him, as certain women sometimes are by the faint reminding threat of terrible violence in handsome men. He seldom changed his expression, which was concentrated, calm, and aloof, even in those moments he turned and stared at the spectators. Surely these two seemingly ordinary young people—defendant and victim—could have been anybody's children. Could this awful crime have happened anywhere, any time? Why here? And, God, if he truly did this, how could he look so normal? Did he do it? Was he a demon?

Perhaps more than any other state university town in America, Oxford and its people are suffused with and shaped by Ole Miss. It is the third smallest town in the United States which is site of a historic, capstone state university. The campus is only several blocks from the courthouse square; the town and the university are bonded both physically and emotionally. Anything that touches on Ole Miss touches too on the town. The sadness and exhilaration of youth, the innocence of it and even its destructiveness, the vulnerability and recklessness of youth, the transience of the young as they come and go here every four or five years, are quintessential to the town and integral to its character. The tragedy earlier in that spring of five Chi Omegas killed and eleven injured in a freakish accident during a charity "walkathon" was profoundly felt in the town, and would be for a long time, as long as people remember. These girls were our progeny. The five neat and well-kept crosses on Highway 6 were daily reminders that the indwelling sense of immortality in the young, which so beguiles the town itself, is, from Sir Thomas Browne, but "folly and dream of expectation."

The trial for the murder, subject of such hearsay and speculation, horror and enigma, was not long in coming after the deaths and maimings, and was somehow of a piece with the strange, bittersweet sorrow which often pervades small, isolated university towns. As an Ole Miss history professor whose sensibilities I have always trusted told me: "People in Oxford often spoke of our town being different from the rest of America, and the South. It's *safe* here, safe from this kind of wanton barbarism. Then all of a sudden we realized we weren't really different. There was even a bizarre relief in acknowledging this, and we could give in to our curiosity and fascination with this tortured expression of modern man's disorientation."

The families of the two young people sat segregated in the two front pews of the courtroom divided by the middle aisle—parents, siblings, aunts, uncles, cousins. Occasionally they would diffidently glance across at one another. At first, in appearance at least, it seemed unlikely, indeed unfathomable, that their lives had been sundered by brutal death; their later manifestations of grief would put that to the lie. During the shorter recesses, the family of the defendant would retire to the outside balcony at the south side of the room, the victims to the north, the boundary between the two as tangible as the starkest wall.

Two women jurors got sick when the photographs of the girl at the murder house and on the autopsy table were shown them in the jury box. Later, when a forensic expert for the defense displayed the murder pictures on a large projection screen visible not only to the jury but to half the courtroom, the gasp from the spectators was a sharp, palpable exhalation. One afternoon, amid the testimony about drops of blood, bloody towels, and specimens of hair, a springtime Mississippi storm suddenly descended. In seconds the courtroom was in shadows, and to the rumblings of the thunder it began to rain, a dark torrential rainfall accompanied by a heavy wind which tossed the magnolias on the lawn below into anguished contours, as if the very elements were declaring mortification on woebegone humanity.

The young D.A., only a few months in the office, seemed unconfident and tentative at first, but with cross-examinations became more and more effective, displaying a barely contained anger, until before one's eyes he grew progressively as outraged and homespun as Jimmy Stewart (whose antagonist was the wickedly intelligent George C. Scott) in *Anatomy of a Murder.* He grew up in this trial. He brought in the bed on which the defendant had allegedly slept through the night. He reconstructed the dimensions and juxtaposition of the living room and bedroom with adhesive tape on the courtroom floors, the jury box, and even the judge's bench. On cross-examination of the young man he brought in the mock trials and practice video-tapings the defendant had undergone in Dallas, and the jury must have perceived in his testimony a calculating coolness.

The defense was superb, parrying the prosecution's relentless accumulation of circumstantial evidence with stringent logic and sharp thrusts of doubt. But "the twelve men good and true" saw differently.

The jury was out for just over two hours. Two of them were crying when they suddenly returned. The verdict: Guilty of Capital Murder. In one swift moment, the sheriff had the young man in handcuffs and out the back door. It remained for the victim's family to shake hands with and embrace the D.A.

In the punishment phase the next day, the same jury under state law deliberating death or life, it was as if the courtroom itself had undergone the most histrionic transformation. Defense and prosecution spoke in quiet, almost reverential tones. The defendant's family seemed to have suffered an actual physical collapse, to have shrunk in size, shoulders hunched and in tears. It was heart-wrenching. On the stand parents, brother, friends entreated the jury for his life. His mother wept: "*Please . . . mercy.*" The jury could not reach a unanimous verdict; the judge automatically gave the sentence of life.

The courtroom emptied. On the lawn outside: a moving scene. The fathers of defendant and victim briefly converged—whispers exchanged, the elder Hodgkin weeping.

Moments later, we saw young Hodgkin, surrounded by a phalanx of deputies, being escorted on foot across the lawn and up North Lamar to the jail. The crime had seized the town and wrung it out, and now the young man convicted of it was receding from it as inexorably as a pebble in a pond, walking away from us into a bitter future. Soon he disappeared around the corner. He would leave the town in its benumbed calm now, and with the despairing question: Ought not someone somehow have been able to do something? To save her? To save him from himself? His destination was Parchman, and he would be there for many years.

39

Anybody's Children

Mitch and the Infield Fly Rule

Detail from *Aqua Garden—Fish and Flowers*

W hen I first came down to Ole Miss a few years back to be "writer-in-residence," I taught a course on the modern American novel. The English Department picked out for me, they reported, seventy-five of the best students at the university. We met twice a week in a sizeable lecture hall built like an amphitheater.

The reading list, I shall say, was substantial but somewhat eclectic. I had designed it to bring down a few authors. William Styron, John Knowles, and Gloria Jones (James Jones' widow) came free of charge to discuss *Sophie's Choice, A Separate Peace,* and *From Here to Eternity,* and so did George Plimpton, Jack Whitaker, and Michael Burke to talk about their friendships with novelists.

It was heady fare. One afternoon, in the middle of my lecture on *Go Down, Moses,* from the back of the hall I heard an ungodly noise—a kind of exaggerated yawn, a plaintive cry of ennui and exasperation. My God, I thought, I'm boring them to death. It turned out, however, to be my black Labrador Pete, who had come into the room before I had arrived and was sleeping on the floor of the back row.

Ole Miss has forever been noted for its beautiful coeds. It has had several Miss Americas, and I will confess there were quite a few lovely girls in that class. They served to encourage the Socratic method. On fine spring days they would arrive en masse in shorts and halters and sit on the front rows, unmercifully tormenting their middle-aging teacher; sometimes my dog Pete came in with them. The most beautiful of all was a willowy, full-breasted blond Chi Omega, twenty-one years old, tall and slender and lithesome with a throaty Bacall voice, wry and irreverent and whimsical, a fount of good cheer. And a straight-A student! We called her "Mitch." I had given her a 96 on her report on Walker Percy's *The Moviegoer*. She told me she identified with the troubled male protagonist, Binx Bolling of New Orleans. I should not even have to write this: I was secretly in love with her, of course.

I had Mark Harris' novel of baseball and death, *Bang the Drum Slowly,* on the reading list. I tried unsuccessfully to get Mark Harris himself to journey down, and then on impulse I asked Jake Gibbs, the Ole Miss baseball coach who had spent ten years as a catcher with the Yankees, to lecture on the book.

"You say it's about a catcher?" Jake asked as he spit a little Levi Garrett under the bleachers during practice.

I told him yes, and even added that he would not have to deal with symbolism or divine any existentialist meaning. But Jake had a home doubleheader on the appointed day against Boo Ferriss' Delta State University club and declined the invitation, with considerable relief, I sensed.

On the night before the class, I was sitting at the bar of the Warehouse off the courthouse square and sighted Mitch at a table with friends. I asked her to join me for a minute.

"What is it, Prof?" she asked.

"How would you like to earn a bottle of ice-cold Moët & Chandon?" I said.

She glanced at me apprehensively. "What do I have to do?"

"You've got a good memory. Just memorize this word for word and quote it when I call on you tomorrow." I furtively withdrew from my coat *The Sporting News'* pocket-sized *Official Baseball Rules* and pointed to a section on page eighteen.

"What is it?" she said, looking down.

"The infield fly rule."

"The *what*?"

No need for questions, I said. "Just memorize it. And remember that the reason for the rule is that an infielder in this situation could drop the ball on purpose and then turn an easy double play." She asked me to repeat this rationale, then promised to be ready.

It was a pristine afternoon for baseball. The windows of the lecture hall were open to let in the honeyed scents of Deep Southern April. The baseball field was across the street, and we could hear the sounds of bat-on-ball and the roar of the crowd in the soft, languid sunshine.

I gave my lecture on *Bang the Drum Slowly,* then asked questions. Mr. Bill Rhodes of Indianola had just addressed himself well to a singular irony: the catcher got better and better the closer he came to death. Yet death itself seemed a chimera on this matchless day of spring.

Five minutes remained in the class when I posed the last question.

"Who can identify the infield fly rule?" I asked.

"The *what*?" one of the coeds said.

"Infield fly rule."

There was an awkward, deepening silence among the Ole

Miss scholars. Then a big old boy from the Delta raised his hand.

"Mr. Edwards."

"With runners on first and third with two outs, if the batter. . . ."

"Wrong. Anyone else?"

A smart black Ole Miss Rebel basketball player from Memphis now raised his hand: "With runners on second and third and only one out. . . ."

"Wrong again," I said. "*Anyone*?"

They whispered embarrassedly among themselves.

"They tell me you're the best students in all of the University of Mississippi—and not a single one of you can recite the infield fly rule."

After a further pause, from the front row there was another hand. Mitch was wearing blue shorts and a crimson halter. She reminded me in that instant of Candice Bergen in *Carnal Knowledge*.

"Miss Mitchell," I said.

In her deep, lilting Dixie voice she replied, enunciating each word: "An infield fly is a fair fly ball—not including a line drive nor an attempted bunt—which can be caught by an infielder with ordinary effort, when first and second, or first, second, and third bases are occupied, before two are out. The pitcher, catcher, and any outfielder who stations himself in the infield on the play shall be considered infielders for the purpose of this rule."

A cataclysmic rustle filled the big room. Everyone was gazing at her in astonishment. She continued:

"When it seems apparent that a batted ball will be an infield fly, the umpire shall immediately declare 'Infield Fly,' for the benefit of the runners. The ball is alive and runners may advance at the risk of being caught, or retouch and advance after the ball is touched, the same as on any fly ball."

"That's good, Miss Mitchell."

"Wait. I'm not finished."

"Of course. Continue."

"On the infield fly rule the umpire is to rule whether the ball could *ordinarily* have been handled by an infielder—not by some arbitrary limitation such as the grass, or the base lines. The infield fly is in no sense to be considered an appeal play. The umpire's judgment must govern, and the decision should be made immediately."

From the back of the hall students were standing up to get a better view of her as she recited. "I can't believe this," one young man exclaimed.

"What is the reason for this rule?" I asked.

"Perfectly simple," she replied. "An infielder in this situation could drop the ball on purpose and then turn an easy double play. I always thought this a fine rule."

At that very moment the bell sounded. As Mitch left, the crowd parted to let her through. I believe they wanted to touch the hem of her garment—the crimson halter.

I caught up with her alone just beyond Bondurant Hall. "How about a bottle of Moët & Chandon at the Warehouse, Mitch?"

"How about two?" she said.

Capote
Remembered

ruman was my neighbor on eastern Long Island for many years. It was a placid neighborhood of old villages and frosty inlets and ponds full of wild duck and Canada geese and flat, verdant potato fields which swept to the sand dunes and the ocean—a settled place touched with the past. He had a secluded house, hidden behind tall hedges, not far from the Atlantic in Wainscott. He was so often alone.

I lived on Church Lane in Bridgehampton, only two or three miles away. It was the 1970s and I had left New York City. You will often find Southerners in faraway Northern places like Bridgehampton, especially the artists, and their tendency is often to congregate, out of old shared instincts. Usually it is not that they have turned their backs on their native region—far from it. But where does memory best flourish? The imagination? The sharp, sequestered beauty of the great Eastern littoral provides for some the release and detachment so often elusive back home. It is perhaps a matter of personal choice, and of psychic balance.

I had a wonderful black Lab named Pete. Pete and I are strolling up the sidewalk on the main street of Bridgehampton. An enormous Buick with a small man, so small that his nose barely rises above the dashboard, as in the "Kilroy Was Here" drawings of World War II, stops before us.

"Willie! Pete! Hop in and let's ride around and *gossip.*"

Pete gets in back, I in front. "Boys, I can't wait to tell you about my conversation at lunch in Le Côte Basque with Princess Radziwill yesterday." He gestures dramatically and pays little attention to the road.

We are around the block and toward the ocean. Finally we are travelling in long widening circles around the dunes and potato fields. Truman is telling us of his social life in Manhattan, a brilliant, perfervid monologue touched with flamboyant dervishes and irreverent pirouettes. Now he is talking of Bennett and Phyllis Cerf—some party for a U. S. Senator—and Babe Paley in the Four Seasons, and a tryst in a New Jersey motel between a WASP female socialite and a mobster. And a lunch in the Plaza, I think with Kay Graham. In the back seat Pete is scratching a flea: Truman is talking about the Princess again.

"How old were you when you wrote *Other Voices, Other Rooms*?" I interrupt.

He pauses over the dashboard. "So very young," he says. "Oh so very young and brilliant."

He negotiates the turn at Church Lane. He tells me of his latest recipe for quiche. "Oh, Willie," he says. "How naive you are! Your simplicity! The things I could tell you!"

Nearly four years after his death in the cool confines of Joanne Carson's house in Beverly Hills, Truman was back in the news. In May 1988, Simon and Schuster brought out a major Capote biography by Gerald Clarke, a biography that followed on the heels of publication of *The Truman Capote Reader* and *Answered*

Prayers—or at least the bits and pieces of *Answered Prayers* that the scholars and the literary grave diggers have been able to find. Truman would have been amused by it all. He always did understand the spotlight, perhaps better than the rest of us. *Answered Prayers* was to have been Truman's great novel, and the promise of it kept attention focused on him even in those later years when he was known by many people more for the words that came out of his mouth than the words that ended up on the printed page.

There were many words that came out of that mouth, of course. From the articles that have appeared since Truman's death, I suppose it is obvious that in his last days he was beclouded by drugs and booze. The declining days of fine writers—especially, I think, in America—bring on the interviewers; these last days are painful and lonely, and they are too often the days that are remembered. I suspect that the trauma of writing *In Cold Blood*—those long years spent in the company of killers—was what led Truman to drugs and eventually damaged the soul of the boy who wrote *A Christmas Memory*. But for all the sad glimpses of him in his latter, suffering days that the books and the biographies and the excerpts give us, I prefer to remember another Truman, one I shared food and time and talk with on the shores of the island. This is the same Truman I still meet when I pull his books from my shelves. This is, I like to believe, the true Truman, the one that refuses to be obscured by gossip—even his own.

I liked Truman, and, for whatever reason, he liked me. I don't know if this mutual affection was because we were both small town Southerners in a place where there were few of us to be found. It may well be so; the small town South never left Truman, though it always seemed subtly at war with his cosmopolitan instincts. When I first got to know him, I suspected he had given too much of his heart's core to those cosmopolitan instincts, to a style of living and a company of companions about whom he cared too much, a company that chose to turn upon him in his twilight time.

Truman may well not have agreed. Though he was very small, and he had that high, shrill, lispy voice, touched by the South, that was as distinctive a voice as I ever heard (there is no way to mimic the way he talked, although even those of us who cared for him tried when he was not around), he claimed he was impervious to bullying. The other children never bullied him when he was growing up, he said, because he had the most wicked tongue in town; the adults he later seemed a child among likely never bullied him for the same reason.

Truman's voice came from his past as a solitary orphan brought up by old maid Alabama cousins, from his life as the kid who started writing and getting drunk on wine at age twelve. The immemorial Christmas morning in Alabama was an indelible part of him—as was the dual hanging in the state prison in Kansas he captured in *In Cold Blood*. These were the two poles of Truman's art—observing himself and observing others.

I cannot help but believe that both poles had much to do with his raising in the ornately polite society that was so often found in the old small town South, a society that rewarded you well for keen observation and encouraged a child to listen. Truman did listen. He could hear what people said, and what they meant, and then get that on paper in a clear and clean way that escapes most writers. Other writers could not help but envy in Truman that which, if he had been a singer, might have been called his purity of tone.

But that purity may well have been a curse as well as a charm. When I grew to know Truman on Long Island, Southern boys sharing a familiarity of knowledge, I wondered if perhaps the keenness of his observation had begun to wear on him. What he could put on paper was never quite as true as what he could see, and so there were long periods in which he published little, and the constant unmet promise of *Answered Prayers*. Truman could talk what he saw, could keep the audience at bay with the wicked intelligence of his tongue, but though he may have archly realized that all literature is gossip, he knew as well that all gossip is not literature. As he got older, he found it harder to write, he said, because his standards were too high. It was easier when he was twenty-five, but at fifty he expected too much of himself. For all his fame from conversation, Truman realized he was a writer. But he was a writer who had to meet the hard standards of an acerbic critic whose last name was Capote.

My mother died in Mississippi, and I was staying for a month or so in the Yazoo Motel settling the tiny estate when I saw in the papers that Truman was giving the main lecture at the Mississippi Arts Festival in Jackson the next afternoon. I needed to get out of town.

I drove the forty-odd miles to Jackson and arrived a few minutes early, posting myself at the back stage entrance to the auditorium on the Millsaps campus.

Momentarily a large limousine pulled up. Truman was in it, surrounded by several literary matrons in hats. He was looking glum—*trapped* may be a better word—and was perhaps rather drunk. Then suddenly he sighted me, and his expression was transmuted.

"There's Willie Morris!" he shouted. "Oh, boy!"

He embraced me, an inebriated little bear dressed up for a literary reading. "What in the *world* are *you* doing here?" Afterwards, in the bar of his motel, the lady and her handsome young daughter who were accompanying him the next day to Los Angeles (he was trying to get the young daughter a modeling job in Beverly Hills) left us to our talk.

A middle-aged woman with purple hair from Alabama came to our table.

"Mr. Capote, I read that book *In Cold Blood*. I just have one question. Did you personally know them two *murderers*?"

"Madame," he said, "did I know them? I lived with them for seven *years*."

In his motel room that night, before I left to drive back to Yazoo City, he lay on the bed drinking straight from a fifth of Smirnoff. The young model held a cold washrag on his head. She took me to a corner of the room and whispered: "Where did he get that bottle?" Then she returned to the bed. "Try to get some sleep, Truman," she said.

"*Sleep!*" he said. "Two thousand people heard me today for five grand. And this man's momma died. And you say *sleep*?"

In his final days, he would come into a bar on Long Island called Bobby Van's to drink and pass out. Bobby's was the gathering spot for the painters and writers who had come to the vicinity over the years, and for the local people who joined us there in bemused comradeship—a mahogany bar and Tiffany lamps, checkered tablecloths, and a baby grand on which

Bobby often played Cole Porter and Gershwin tunes. Sometimes Truman started drinking at noon, other times in late afternoon or early evening. Usually, he was by himself.

The cops were always picking him up for DWIs, expired licenses, and unregistered cars. There were dents in his big Buick. In his lucid moments, he would talk with us of his most dramatic conflicts with people. He had turned on those who owned yachts. The big rich did not answer their own prayers. When four excerpts from *Answered Prayers*—a roman à clef of the rich and powerful with names and addresses unchanged—appeared in *Esquire,* his former friends had spurned him.

Those of us who cared for Truman had something of a proprietary feeling for him. I think we felt his extraordinary tenderness and self-destructive vulnerability, and we worried a little for him, for he often seemed lost and afraid. I drove him home from Bobby Van's a number of times. One heard the roar of the ocean from his house. He would sit in an enormous sofa much too big for him. One afternoon of snow and high winds he brought out an unopened pint of seventy-five-year-old bourbon that he said he had bought at an auction for $300. When I took a sip, I could feel it in my toes. Truman drank most of it, and it enhanced his stories. But as the stories wound down, he would sink into his sofa, a small man, alone. "I have too many houses in too many places," he would complain then, and he would number his various establishments on his fingers. When I admired one of his paperweights on the coffee table, he said: "Isak Dinesen gave it to me. It's yours. Please." I refused. "If not, never speak to me again." He gave wristwatches to people he trusted, he said. Why not paperweights?

The last time I was with him was at a noontime Sunday of early spring in Bobby Van's. The lilacs were out, and Bill Styron and I were at the bar when Truman came in alone and took his front table at the window overlooking the sidewalk. Bill and I went to pay our respects.

"Lunch is on me," Truman said. "Pull up a chair."

He was at his best—funny, charming, and effusive. He was glad to see us, and he regaled us with stories. He was close to finishing *Answered Prayers,* he said, between his vodkas. He was in the middle of a memoir for *Playboy,* he told us, of his late friend and adversary Tennessee Williams. He had just finished a paragraph that morning about Tennessee, he said, and he began to quote it to us. As he talked, I was reminded of an earlier moment, also in Bobby Van's, but with James Jones at my side instead of Styron. In the dying sunlight, Jones and I had sat mesmerized as Truman, in his wide-brimmed hat, began telling us, in the most graphic detail, all about his family from Alabama. I had never once heard him open himself so like that, about his parents, aunts, uncles, cousins, and himself there in the South. We learned that his mother had once been "Miss Alabama" years before she committed suicide, and that one of his cousins was a professional parachute jumper. To some, it may have seemed incongruous that the lisping little fellow with the wide-brimmed hat could talk so easily, so comfortably with the supposedly macho, busted-down sergeant James Jones about Alabamian aunts and uncles—and about his time in the French Quarter in New Orleans, and the months he spent in the motel room in Garden City, Kansas. And it may have seemed equally incongruous that Jones would listen. But there was nothing extraordinary about the easy conversation;

the men who wrote *In Cold Blood* and *The Thin Red Line* knew mutually of life's shadings and extremes.

Remembering now that last time, when Truman shared his table with a boy from Mississippi and a boy from Virginia, I understand the truth of what Styron later said about our host: "Here was an artist of my age who could make words dance and sing, change color mysteriously, perform feats of magic, provoke laughter, send a chill up the back, touch the heart—a full-fledged master of the language before he was old enough to vote." I also understand the truth of what Truman once told me in Bobby Van's: "All Southerners go home sooner or later," he said, "even if in a box."

Truman did not make it in the box; his ashes now rest in Long Island. But I feel that on that afternoon in Bobby Van's he had already returned home. He was telling stories, alive to the power of the word, living the life he had learned in Monroeville, Alabama. I wish to remember Truman in just this way—the exuberant, witty, brave, and outrageous observer of the human parade in its foibles, of the people passing by. That is the true Truman Capote, the one that no tawdry memoirs or tales of dissolution can diminish, the one that readers meet every time they examine the finely honed phrases of "A Tree of Night" or "Children On Their Birthdays." That was Truman Capote the writer, my friend, and a man I miss.

59

My Two Oxfords

I am a singular creature, among the handful who has dwelled for any length of time in two of the world's disparate places—the Oxford in England and the Oxford in Mississippi. On the one hundred fiftieth anniversary of the founding of the Mississippi one, I address myself to the subject. May I suggest there are similarities, but not all that many?

Still, it has always struck me as poignant that the white settlers who first came to this spot in the red hills of northeast Mississippi in the 1820s and 1830s, cleared the piney woods and made churches and roads and schools and jails and had a courthouse square for themselves by the time of the Civil War (everything being in readiness for Federal General A. J. "Whiskey" Smith to burn it all down in 1864), named their town *Oxford*. They wanted to acquire the new state university to dignify their raw terrain, and they were happy they got it, by a one-vote margin of the legislature.

The namesake is rather more venerable. Its first mention was in the Anglo-Saxon chronicle of 912 A.D., and of the university in the twelfth century, although legend ascribes the origins to Alfred the Great. My own Oxford college, New College, was new in 1379, and God knows what might have been transpiring in the forests and swamp bottoms of Lafayette County, Mississippi, in that auspicious year.

Has any single place on earth of comparable size produced such an august and eclectic array of human beings as the English Oxford? Indulge me this casual list, in random order: Thomas Browne, Samuel Johnson, A. E. Housman, William Penn, John Wesley, William Gladstone, Thomas More, John Locke, Lewis Carroll, Philip Sidney, Edward VII, Cardinal Wolsey, Randolph Churchill, Max Beerbohm, Bishop Wilberforce, Matthew Arnold, Robert Peel, T. S. Eliot, Walter Raleigh, Cecil Rhodes, Cecil Day-Lewis, Lord Bryce, Christopher Wren, William Blackstone, Lord Salisbury, Percy Bysshe Shelley, Clement Attlee, Joseph Addison, Richard Steele, Oscar Wilde, Edward Gibbon, John Galsworthy, Charles James Fox, Siegfried Sassoon, Thomas Hobbes, Admiral Blake, Evelyn Waugh, Walter Pater, General Haig, Lawrence of Arabia, Charles Lyell, Lord Baltimore, Cardinal Newman, Arnold Toynbee, Adam Smith, Robert Southey, Algernon Charles Swinburne, Quiller-Couch, Thomas De Quincey, Lord Asquith, Lord Grey of Fallodon, King Olav of Norway, Prince Felix Youssoupoff, who assassinated Rasputin, and General Fridelin von Singer, who commanded the German forces at Monte Cassino. This is a mere sampling, but imagine the oppressiveness of their footfalls as their spirits stalked a callow young American there a generation ago.

I lived almost four years in the classic Oxford in the late 1950s. I came down from New York to the Mississippi Oxford in 1980 to be writer-in-residence at the University of Mississippi and I have been here ever since. Was it the call of the name? Was there something in the blood compelling one to risk assimilating these most dissimilar landscapes? As with other of the curious and divergent experiences of a lifetime, can the two Oxfords be assimilated at all? Or are they both to me a dream?

Certainly that other Oxford is dreamlike to me now in its unfolding, a Lewis Carroll fantasy for a golden summer's afternoon. From the summit of the years I find it difficult to conceive I was actually there. Does this seem strange? Surely it was the first and last time I would ever live in a museum. Its spires and cupolas and quadrangles, its towers and gables and oriels and hieroglyphs, its ancient walls with the shards of glass embedded on top, its chimes and bells resounding in the swirling mists, made home seem distant and unreal. I lived in frigid rooms overlooking a spacious Victorian quadrangle, a stone's throw across the greensward from a massive twelfth century wall with turrets and apertures for arrows. A boys choir sang madrigals every afternoon from the somber chapel across the way. I dined in a gloomy medieval hall with its portraits of parliamentarians and ecclesiastics, warriors and kings. The dons at first were as terrifying to me as nuns in my childhood.

The sacrosanct privacy of the place, the perpetual fogs and rains, elicited a loneliness, an angst and melancholia such as I had never before known. The mementos of death were everywhere, in the ubiquitous graveyards, in the interminable rolls of the war dead in the chapels. The spirit of Kipling and Rupert Brooke resided amidst these scrolls to the fallen young. It was "the City of Dreaming Spires," and "the Home of Lost Causes." The burden of the past was ominous and incontrovertible. The college gates were padlocked at midnight, and within our forbidding fortress we were at the mercy of the ghosts of the centuries, and a squinty-eyed mystic from New Delhi peregrinated in the doomed hours conjuring all of them. After four years at a huge American state university—the final one as editor of the largest student daily in the United States—the change

65

My Two Oxfords

was horrendous. I began spending considerable time in the pubs with the Australians. Emerging from the Turf Tavern one foggy late afternoon into a secret medieval walkway which led to the college, we happened upon a curious assemblage: elves and fairies and Elizabethan princes and princesses and a girl in white robes playing a flute. "I had too bloody much *this* time," the Aussie from Brewarrina, New South Wales, said, unaware that the college drama club had just finished a Shakespearean rehearsal.

Lectures were optional. One of the English students explained to me that they had gone out of vogue with the invention of the printing press in the fifteenth century. Examinations were comprehensive and came at the end of three years. The tutorial system was the core of the Oxford education. Students wrote weekly or twice-weekly essays and discussed them in private sessions with the dons.

I remember my first essay. The tutor, Herbert Nicholas, had assigned me the Reform Act of 1832. I read seven or eight books and perused a half dozen others. I stayed up all night polishing my effort to a thundering conclusion. Before a gentle fire in the don's rooms above the college gardens I read the next-to-last sentence. "Just how close the people of England came to revolution in 1832 is a question we shall leave with the historians," and was about to move on to the closing statement. "But Morris," interrupted the tutor, "we *are* the historians."

With the essays the only formal requirement, one might do as he pleased: read novels, write poetry, walk along the river, sleep till noon, go to London, bicycle through the Cotswolds, or spend sixteen hours a day reading for the next tutorial. A

West Point man claimed he went to the bulletin board near the tower-gateway twice a day looking for an order telling him what to do. The community did not judge, nor interfere with, one's personal habitudes. In fads and eccentricities, as in the paths the mind took, the Oxford student was protected by a subtle yet pervasive tolerance. There was an abiding homage there to independence and self-sufficiency, to intellectual candor, to one's own intensely private inclinations.

The paradox and variety of the place were vivid in its social life. There were social functions right out of Edwardian Oxford—from sherry in a don's rooms on Sunday morning to the raucous society dinners with their several courses and four or five wines. On one such evening W. H. Auden, brandishing a large carafe of red wine, wagered me a one-pound note that he could consume the contents in less than a minute. He did so, then collapsed on the floor. There were the fabulous commemoration balls on the college lawns with the all-night champagne, the tables laden with turkey and goose and pheasant and beef and fish and caviar, and the London society orchestras playing through the dusk-like lingering midsummer nights. At twilight one evening in the college cloisters, the guests, ranging from recent graduates to lords and ladies of the realm, sipped champagne and heard the madrigals sung by the boys choir. There was a time, also, for pork pie and inexpensive sherry at someone's lodgings—the Saturday night parties given by the working-class students where, in one or two close and smoky rooms, dozens of undergraduates were crowded inescapably together. Here invariably was a white wine concoction, American jazz from the gramophone, the shy and awkward English talk between boy and girl.

All this has been hard for me to fit into the whole of my American life, and I am no exception. A number of other American writers, from Robert Penn Warren to Reynolds Price, have studied over the years in Oxford, England, but by and large they have not written very much about it. It was an exotic interlude, and I remember it with affection and love and fulfilment and no little bemusement.

Oxford, England, is likewise a commercial and industrial center of well over 100,000 people. Oxford, Mississippi, minus the university students, is an unhurried courthouse-square hamlet of about 11,000, surrounded by a rough and authentic rural countryside. In physical aspect my latter Oxford is closer to the more pastoral Cambridge, without its aura of age or its majestic colleges. Of all the towns and cities in America which are home to the historic, capstone state universities, this Oxford is the third smallest, just behind Orono, Maine, and Vermillion, South Dakota.

Ole Miss is small, too, by measure with other state universities, with slightly more than 9,000 students who are suffused with the flamboyant élan of their American state university contemporaries everywhere. Indeed, unlike the historic Oxford of my past, I find too *little* loneliness here. The emphasis is on gregariousness. The Greek system is strong and entrenched and dominates the social and political life. The rich sorority girls drive baby-blue Buicks with Reagan-Bush bumper stickers. They are noted for their beauty and their gossipy style. Many of them major in "Fashion Merchandising," an intellectual pursuit absent from the curricula of Oxford, England. Their social life is elaborate, organized, and not especially introspective. A New York writer described the rituals of the sorority rush week: "What screams, what cries, what an amplitude of passion. The proceedings are more exotic than the Romsiwarmnavian rites of the primitive Shirentes of Brazil's rain forest." Yet the legendary beauty of the Ole Miss coed is not myth. The girls of Oxford, England, so stringently screened by some of the world's most demanding academic requirements, were often dour; yet the occasional warm-spirited beauty among them was always worth the waiting, and these were the girls, I am pleased to say, that the Yanks got. By the same token, the intellectual Ole Miss sorority girl of good and gentle disposition is a joyous song in the heart, and will endure.

Surely it would be frivolous and indeed self-defeating to compare the students of one of Western civilization's greatest and most ancient institutions with those of a small, isolated Deep Southern American university. Yet in moments there is a palpable, affecting sophistication to this stunningly beautiful campus in the midst of the rolling rural woodlands of the American South. In the juxtaposition of town and school many have been reminded of the Chapel Hill of a generation or so ago, which bustles so now within the perimeters of the Research Triangle. It has so lost its touch with the Carolina land. One often recalls at Ole Miss Thomas Wolfe's description of his only slightly fictional Pulpit Hill years ago in *Look Homeward, Angel:* "There was still a good flavor of the wilderness about the place—one felt its remoteness, its isolated charm. It seemed to Eugene like a provincial outpost of great Rome: the wilderness crept up to it like a beast."

Ole Miss ranks high on the list of American Rhodes Scholars, and as with all state universities there will always be its cadre of bright, imaginative, and hard-working young. Gerald Turner, the resourceful new chancellor who is the youngest in the history of the Mississippi Oxford, wishes to build on the sturdier traditions. Turner has succeeded in a $40 million fund-raising campaign to improve faculty salaries and the library at the university of the poorest state in the Union, and to strike a more wholesome balance between the Greek and independent students, and to stand fast with the First Amendment.

Nowhere is the contrast between the undergraduate life of the two Oxfords more striking than in two enduring institutions of these different locales: the Junior Common Rooms and the Hoka. The *"J.C.R.'s"* of the colleges of Oxford, England, were the traditional student retreats for relaxation and conversation. These were sedate and proper places with frayed carpets and overstuffed Victorian furniture where one retired for tea and crumpets or to read *The Times* or *The Guardian* or the *TLS*. Women were not allowed (in the English Oxford of my era the colleges were rigorously segregated between the sexes) and the repartee was—shall one suggest?—restrained. In the quiet and civilized gloom one would gaze out the windows at the darkening mists or the incessant rain. I was the only person who read there the *Paris Herald-Trib* for the baseball scores. If time weighed too heavily on my contemporaries and me in this setting, we might retire at pub-time to a little oasis of tranquility called the Turf Tavern—an ancient inn accessible only by a narrow medieval passage and presided over by two old maid sisters and their soporific cats—for warm ale around its stone and timbered bars. Here Thomas Hardy's Jude the Obscure courted Arabella the barmaid, but that was before our day.

The Hoka of the Mississippi Oxford, named after the tenacious Chickasaw princess, is situated across an alleyway from a bar reconverted from an old cotton gin. One is witness in this boondocks avant-garde coffeehouse to the true variety of Ole Miss and Oxford life, as opposed to the enclaves of Sorority and Fraternity Rows. It is presided over by Ron Shapiro, a much beloved St. Louis transplant, a kind of white Jewish Rastaman, and one Jim Dees, a Deltan who writes essays under the nom-de-plume "Dr. Bubba." The auditorium in back will have the classic European and American movies. Up front B. B. King will be on the stereo, or the Grateful Dead, or Hank Williams, or Elvis. The Memphis and Jackson newspapers are there on the counter, just as the London papers were in the New College J.C.R. So, however, are vintage issues of *Playboy* and *Field and Stream* and the *Yazoo City Herald,* and a wicked journal called *Southeastern Conference Football.* The patrons will include black athletes, willowy sorority beauties, nocturnal professors, a few carpenters or truck drivers or hairdressers from town, tousled student intellectuals in from a lecture by William Styron or Alex Haley or Eudora Welty or C. Vann Woodward, a black and white softball team, attractive female pharmacy students dining on Hoka chef's salad sprinkled with Dixie herbs and seeds, young editors who have just put the student paper to bed, a defrocked fraternity man or two sitting in a corner writing poems, a group of Ole Miss men recently returned from frog-gigging in the Tallahatchie River bottoms who smell of frogs, legal secretaries of both races from the courthouse square, a table of black sorority girls talking football, law students discussing torts and civil liberties, graduate history students arguing the Wilmot Proviso, the writer Barry Hannah between books, and an invariable blend of foreign students trying to make something of the perfervid and eclectic dialogue. One recent evening I joined two black and two white South Africans engaged in heartfelt, almost brotherly talk of their tragic nation.

Two or three of the village dogs will wander in expecting a sampling of the cheese nachos or a nibble from the most popular sandwich of the place, called mysteriously "The Love at First Bite." Instead of tea and crumpets, here there are cinnamon coffee, bagels, and New Orleans-style *beignets*. The mood is mischievous but well-behaved, and some of the soliloquies are lyrical. On the walls are posters and circulars announcing rock concerts in the Delta, or blues festivals in the darkest canebrakes, indigenous sculptures, and photographs of Mississippi's writers. There are portraits, too, of Vietnam veterans by a talented young photographer. In the girls' restroom, I am told, there is graffiti too graphic for the toilets of St. Hilda's College, Oxford, England. Yet, as with the English J.C.R.'s, in its own mode this, too, is an honorable place, where words matter yet.

A casual stroll through the English Oxford of my youth would lead one, of course, to some of the impressive landmarks and monuments of the western world. Many was the afternoon I toured the town and countryside alone, or with a favorite English girl, or with visitors from home, absorbing its fleeting grey auras. The winding High Street or St. Aldate's or the Broad was always crowded with the red double-decked buses, bicycles, and trams, and the sidewalks with the townspeople and the undergraduates in their odd truncated academic gowns.

There were the sudden cul-de-sacs and alleyways, the Broad Walk with its avenue of towering elms, the fragrance and intense greenery of spring along the Isis or Cherwell. The afternoon offered limitless possibilities: the lavish interiors of the college chapels and the serene college gardens, the eerie facade of Mob Quad of Merton dating to the early fourteenth century, the grandeur and sweep of Tom Quad in Christ Church, the Crown Tavern near Carfax frequented by Shakespeare, the Georgian houses along Beaumont Street, the grotesque sixteenth century gargoyles in the Magdalen Cloisters, the Martyr's Memorial in front of Balliol with the statues of the doomed Cranmer, Ridley and Latimer, the regency elegance of St. John's Street, the opulence and isolation of Trinity, the self-proclaimed splendor of Rhodes House, the wonderful private retreat of Blackwell's Book Store where the clerks left you alone as you browsed through Gibbon or Macaulay. One might pause in the Bodleian to look at the first editions of Chaucer or Shakespeare or Milton, or in the Ashmolean for its timeless collections. Or one might tarry in a favorite pub and eavesdrop on discourses about Toynbean cycles, French existentialism, the foreign policy of the United States, or the latest debate in the House of Commons. How I grew to love these walks of my youth in the noble, heroic old town! And touching everything on this day would be the omniscient, indwelling past.

A similar afternoon's tour of the Mississippi Oxford will be another study in catastrophic contrasts. Foremost are the Faulknerian landmarks. Beginning at the courthouse square with its Confederate soldier facing southward and the benches on the lawn crowded with sunburnt men chewing tobacco, one will follow the shady, settled streets with the antebellum houses hidden in magnolias or crepe myrtles. Their names are Shadow Lawn, Rowan Oak, Memory House. One may stroll by the oldest domicile in town, which was built in 1830. In front of the jail aged white and black men wearing Ole Miss baseball caps sit in haphazard conversation. The Ole Miss students speed by in their cars, their shouts and laughter trailing behind them, and there will be dusty pickups with farmers in khakis from Beat Four. The sorority girls have been in their rooms on campus painting their toenails, when one of them shouts: "Anybody want to go buy some *shoes*?" Everything is a blend of the town and the enveloping, untouched country.

The campus will be only a few blocks down University Avenue. Here the town and the university come together. In the bowers and groves lush with dogwood and forsythia in the spring, white and black students sit together under the trees, or drift languidly toward their classrooms. The old Lyceum is at the crest of the hill, and the library with its inscription: "I believe that man will not merely endure . . . he will prevail." Not far from here is the football stadium, where 40,000 people—four times more than the population of the town—will unquietly congregate on the autumnal afternoons.

The differences between my two Oxfords are even more emphatic in their countrysides. The miniature Oxfordshire country beyond the factories and modest brick homes of the industrial workers is one of manicured landscapes, tiny rivers, stone walls and cottages and comforting greens, ancient parish churches and crumbling graveyards and manor houses at the horizon, perfect vegetable and flower gardens, and pristine village streets with antique shops and tea houses. In any direction from the campus or the courthouse square of the Mississippi Oxford, a two-mile drive or less, is the rough red earth, hard and unrelenting. Black and white farmers amble along the roads. The dark, snake-infested kudzu vines are everywhere, the landscape dotted with creeks and swamps and abandoned wooden houses, and country dogs bay in the distance. In the fields are scraggly cotton and soybeans, and on the horizon are the violent rains and windstorms of the Deep South. The rural hamlets of Lafayette County consist of a few derelict stores, a catfish restaurant, a church or two, a miniscule U. S. Post Office with firewood more often than not stacked on the front porch, and an untidy graveyard—"the short and simple annals of the poor." In such terrain at the proper seasons, one might sight more than a few of the male students of Ole Miss, hunting in the swamp bottoms with their dogs. This is the closest equivalent in the Mississippi Oxford to following the hounds and will not invite an especially intimate comparison.

On returning from their countrysides to each of the two Oxfords, the vistas from afar will also be dissimilar. The sight of the English Oxford from a distance is one of the most imposing and unforgettable in Europe. The sun breaks through and catches its silhouettes, its spires and walls and cupolas all in filigree, its gaunt and self-contained fortress aspect, and this exists for me in memory now as an apparition. The vista of the Mississippi Oxford from a high, wooded hill is of the campus half-shrouded in its dense vegetation, and of the twin water towers of town, and always the courthouse.

Finally, each Oxford, indeed, has been a "home of lost causes." In the English Oxford there were the successive changes of religion, the Civil War in which the university declared for the Stuarts and the town for Parliament, the bloody and immemorial political disputes, the executions and public burnings.

Of the Mississippi Oxford, Gerald Turner speaks of the "extraordinary resilience" Ole Miss has shown in its 140-year history.

It too is a place of ghosts. Almost no other American campus envelops death and suffering and blood, and the fire and sword, as Ole Miss does. In the American Civil War it was closed down and became a hospital for both sides. The bloodbath of Shiloh was only eighty miles away. Hundreds of boys of both sides died on the campus, their corpses stacked like cordwood, buried now in unmarked graves in a nearby glade. There is a Confederate statue on the campus also, given to the university by the Faulkners as the one on the courthouse square was. The University Grays, all Ole Miss boys, suffered bitter casualties in that war. One hundred and three of their number were in the first wave of the charge at Gettysburg. Through later poverty and political interference and racial crises the institution somehow survived.

In 1962, John Kennedy dispatched almost 30,000 federalized troops during the riots over the admission of the first black student, James Meredith. As we know all too well, two people were killed and scores injured; it could have been worse. As recently as five years ago, several hundred white students marched on a black fraternity house protesting the abolition of the Confederate flag as a university symbol. In 1982, the university observed the twentieth anniversary of the Meredith confrontation. Interracial audiences gathered for an awards ceremony for distinguished black graduates of Ole Miss and for speeches by blacks and whites. The keynote address was given by Meredith.

Black enrollment at Ole Miss today is just under eight percent, in the American state with the largest black population, thirty-six percent. The black students have sometimes complained that they are left out of the social life of the campus. The Greek system remains completely segregated. The varsity athletic teams are, of course, totally integrated, and the outstanding black athletes are genuine campus heroes. The Ole Miss Rebels football team has the highest ratio of black players in the Southeastern Conference and perhaps the nation—fifty-four percent—and the white-and-black band plays a rendition of "The Battle Hymn of the Republic" and "Dixie" called "From Dixie With Love" at sporting events which would bring tears to the eyes of a Massachusetts abolitionist. The chancellor has pledged to recruit more black students in substantial numbers and to increase black faculty members. One cannot help but note here a new spirit of interracial good will. As Professor David Sansing has written, who would have imagined in those precarious days of 1962 that Ole Miss's most recent Rhodes Scholar would be black, or that the grandson of Mohandis Gandhi would come in 1987 to study race relations in America?

Ultimately, one supposes now, I was only an interloper in the English Oxford. When the moment came, I collected my paraphernalia, mostly books, and returned home again to America. It had been the freest time of my life, and I learned there something of myself—my abilities, faults, convictions, prejudices.

As for the Mississippi Oxford, it lurks forever now in my heart. For it is the heart which shapes my affection for my two Oxfords, and across the years brings them ineluctibly together for me.

A Return to Christmases Gone

Detail from *Ridge Run—Fresh Flowers*

Death in life, life in death,
All of truth in this.
So don't be sad,
Jiggle on your strings.

—ancient French jingle
trans. by W. Morris

The town was so wonderfully contained for me in those Christmases of early childhood that I could hardly have asked for anything else: the lights aglitter in front of the established homes on the hills and down in the flat places, the main street with its decorations stretching away to the bend in the murky river—a different place altogether from the scorched vistas of its summers. The cruelty and madness of adolescence would come later, plenty of time for that. There was an electricity in the very atmosphere then, having to do, I know now, with being little and with pride in the sudden luster, and when we went caroling and gave our Christmas baskets to the poor white people in the neglected apartment houses and the Negroes in the shacks on stilts in the swamp bottoms, on those cool crisp nights after school had turned out for the holidays, I would look into the Delta at the evening star bright and high in the skies and think to myself: There is the Star itself, the one that guided them to the new child. To this day when I hear "O Little Town of Bethlehem," that town for me is really Yazoo. Once, many years later, I sat at a bar on eastern Long Island on Christmas Eve overhearing two Madison Avenue executives as they plotted in vivid and profane detail how to have their boss fired by the first of the year, and I thought: where did it all go?

Where does memory begin? I remember a Christmas pageant in the church when we were five years old. Our teacher had borrowed one of the infant Turner twins to be Jesus, promising the Turners that no one would drop her on the floor. The Baby Jesus himself was never treated so gingerly. They only let us use her in the dress rehearsal and the real evening. Kay King was Mary, I was Joseph, and Bubba Barrier was the innkeeper. When I knocked on the door, Bubba was supposed to open it, thrust his head out, and say, in a booming injunction: *"No room in the inn!"* We had practiced it to adult perfection. But when the night came, Bubba was flustered by the dozens of parents and relatives crowding the church sanctuary. When I knocked on the door of the inn, he opened it with diffidence and said: "Willie, we done run out of space."

For me those mornings of Christmas were warm with the familiar ritual. We would wake up shortly after dawn in our house in Yazoo—my mother, my father, my dog Old Skip, and I. Old Skip would have rousted me out of sleep with his cold wet nose, then pull the blankets off me with his teeth to make sure I did not stay in the bed any longer. No worry about that on *this* day. We would open the presents. My mother would play three or four carols on the Steinway baby grand—then we would have the sparsest of breakfasts to save room for the feast to come. Under the purple Mississippi clouds which, much as I prayed for it, never brought snow, we drove the forty miles south to be with my grandmother, Mamie, my grandfather, Percy, and my two old incorrigible great-aunts, Maggie and Susie, who were born during the Civil War. The drive itself is etched in my heart, the tiny hamlets of the plain where white and black children played outside with their acquisitions of the day, the sad unpainted country stores with the patent medicine posters trimmed in tinsel, and finally the splendid glimpse of the capitol dome and the ride down State Street to the little brick house on North Jefferson. When Old Skip saw the house he would bound out the door like a fox, and I was not far behind.

They would be there on the gallery under the magnolia tree waiting for us, the four of them, and we would all go inside to wild hosannas and exultant embracings to exchange our gifts—modest items for sure, because we were not rich—and examine what we had given each other, and then sit down and catch up on our tidings. And the smells from the kitchen! The fat turkey and giblet gravy and cornbread stuffing and sweet potatoes with melted marshmallows and the nectar and ambrosia and roasted pecans and mincemeat pies. Old Skip hovered around the oven and my two great-aunts bumped into each other every now and again and wished each other Merry Christmas, while the rest of us sank into the chairs by the fire in the parlor and awaited what my grandmother Mamie was making for us. Christmas songs wafted from the chimes of the church down the way, and the crackle of firecrackers came from the neighboring lawns, and my grandmother would dart out of the kitchen with Old Skip at her heels and say: "Almost done now!"

Then, at eleven in the morning, never later, we would sit at the ancient table which had been my great-great-grandmother's: my grandfather Percy and my father at opposite ends, my mother and great-aunts on one side of it, my grandmother and I on the other, Old Skip poised next to my chair expecting his favors. We would sit there for two hours, it seemed, all of them talking about vanished Christmases, and people long since departed from the earth. The clock on the mantle would sound each quarter-hour, and my great-aunts would ask for more servings and say: "My, ain't this *good*?"

I would look around me every year at each of them, and feel Old Skip's nose on my hand, as if all this were designed for me alone. Then, after the rattling of dishes, we would settle in the parlor again, drowsy and fulfilled, and talk away the afternoon. Finally my grandmother, standing before us by the fire, would gaze about the room and always say, in her tone at once poignant and bemused: "Oh, well, another Christmas come and gone."

They themselves are all gone now, each one of them: Mamie and Percy and Maggie and Susie, buried in a crumbling grave-yard on a hill; my mother and father in the cemetery in Yazoo; Old Skip behind the house.

Only I remain, and on Christmases now far away from home, I remember them.

When you drive through the main entrance of the Yazoo cem-etery, make a right at the water fountain near the witch's grave and then a left at the next curve and proceed down this road almost to the end, you will come upon an angel. It will be on your right, only a few feet from the road; you can hardly miss it. It adorns the grave of a little girl. Her name was Maud, and she was five years old when she died in 1921.

I had driven down alone from Oxford the night before. Most of my comrades there are taking the holidays elsewhere, in Florida, or Vermont, or, God forbid, Dallas. It is Christmas morning of 1985, the first Christmas I will spend in the town in almost thirty years; I am to go to a party that night among old friends. When I awakened on Christmas Eve I said to myself, *audibly* as those of us who live more or less by our own devices, will understand: "Either Long Island or Yazoo, but decide quick."

The cemetery at this hour is deserted. A pair of elderly ladies had been dallying at a grave near the entrance, one of them carrying a Christmas wreath, but they have just departed. A solitary man, middle-aged, in a dark suit and tie, had been kneeling before a fresh plot among old stones with the Gregory Funeral Home tent covering it, but he too was gone. Although I am driving to my parents' graves, I am drawn almost as an act of the most fragile subconscious to Maud's angel. I do not quite know why. Perhaps it is because of the photograph I remember, taken by my mother on our ancient fold-out Kodak which my father had given her for Christmas. The picture is now in one of many boxes in my basement at Ole Miss containing the paraphernalia of one's past, and it is of me when I was a child Maud's age, sprawled in the summer's grass in front of the angel. I came across it not too long ago, faded and yellowing at the edges,and it brought back for me the dew of that late summer's day and the crickets chirping from the bayou beyond. Was that forty-five years ago? One faraway afternoon in the rain my young friends and I paused here and saw raindrops like tears dripping from the angel's eyes. "Look!" one of them said. "She's alive! Why is she so sad?" All around me now are the familiar grey tombstones of that childhood time, receding in every direction in the diaphanous mist, and I lean down and touch the angel's wings to remind myself I am the little boy who was there.

I have brought with me a half-dozen red roses, which I bought in the store just off the Oxford Square at closing time on Christmas Eve: "For your girlfriend?" the clerk had asked in a whiskey breath. "No," I replied. "I think for the dead." "Well," he said, "they can use them too." Now I put one of the roses on the grave beneath the angel. I hoped Santa Claus had once been good to Maud.

The new section is straight up the hill, separated from the old by a deep, precipitous ravine, as if a tortuous no-man's land was chosen to divide the two irrevocably, a chasm at once tangible and peremptory between the generations. They began using this vast green hill when I was a boy, and it is almost filled now, the stones stretching away as far as the eye could see. Where will they go from here?

My mother and father are here, under identical stones next to a treacherous side road. Much of a nearby slope has been eroded by the rains, and this adjacent terrain is heavy with desolation and ruin. I walk toward them among the graves of those their age I knew, some of them decorated with holiday flowers—the parents of my contemporaries, the American Legionnaires who sponsored our baseball teams, the grammar school teachers of my day. The whole hill is populated with people I once knew. I try hard to summon their faces. I pause before my parents, thinking of them when I was a child, when they were younger—so hard to conceive—than I am now. On each grave I place a rose, loathing to leave them here on this cheerless morning of the Yuletide.

Then I get into the car, driving down the hill past the untouched woods where I once played echo to the Taps for the military funerals of the Korean dead, and on into town.

The streets on the Delta side are preternaturally quiet. Earlier the children had been playing outdoors with their new toys, but it has begun to rain, a cold, impenetrable rain that has driven them inside. Christmas lights glitter in the gloom.

And here, on Grand Avenue, is the house—*my* house. I park surreptitiously across the street to take a look. I do not even know who lives in it now. But I know every inch of this house; my sweetest dreams and bleakest nightmares are filled with it. It exists in my deepest blood. At this very hour four decades ago we would have been getting ready to go to Jackson.

There are no cars in the driveway, and no lights in the house. I make a U-turn, stop in front, and gaze about me. There are sounds of activity in the Graeber and Norquist and North houses along the street, but not a soul is in sight. I take another rose and get out of the car.

I look into the windows. The parlor seems empty and bereft without my mother's baby grand. My father's easy chair and his big short-wave radio are gone from the side room, filled now with alien furniture. There are no college pennants on the walls of my own room, no battered oak desk, no Corona portable typewriter. The back yard where I had my basketball goal, the grass around it forever dead from our strenuous foot-falls, is strangely neat and manicured. Do no boys live in this house?

It is my heart which tells me where Old Skip is. There is no stone, but no one need show me the patch of earth at the edge of the porch where we wrapped him in my baseball jacket and laid him into the ground. I stand over him in the misty rain. A rose too for the mischievous, affectionate comrade of my boyhood. The residents of our house will return to find it lying incongruously in the winter grass and wonder what interloper might have been here.

I will not be late for the rendezvous in Jackson. I drive up Broadway Hill past the houses which still go by their family names, to the intersection of 49E and W, south through Little Yazoo, Bentonia, Flora, Pocahontas. The road is four-lane now and skirts the little villages, but the countryside is unchanged—the seared kudzu on the tossing hills, the rolling plains beyond the Big Black River, the deep-green pastureland bordering the dark woods. And then Jackson, larger, more sprawling and *metropolitan* than any of us ever dreamed or feared it might become.

I retrace the Christmas journey—down Woodrow Wilson, right on North State past Millsaps, left on Fortification to Jefferson, a whole neighborhood ripped raw of the old places, the service stations and convenience stores mocking me in strict impunity.

My grandparents' house is no longer there, long since a parking lot for the Jitney Jungle across the street. The magnolia is still in front, but where the house was is grim, bare asphalt, cold and wet now from the rain. A stone ledge along the side still remains. It once formed a secret pathway with the house, and I would hide there in the verdant shadows. Just north of the ledge, where Mrs. Dixon's house once stood, they are now building what seems to be a high-rise.

Mamie and Percy, Maggie and Susie would be greeting us now, just beyond the magnolia where the front porch was. I close my eyes and hear their happy welcomes. Old Skip has raced beneath their feet into the house in search of turkey livers, and my great-aunts follow in their flowing black dresses.

I stand alone in the parking lot where the parlor was. I feel the ripple of the lost voices. I drift back into the kitchen. Get away from the oven, Skip! Time as one ages is a continuum. Past and present consume themselves into the ashes. Am I Emily, brought back from the grave in *Our Town*? "I can't bear it," she is reminding me. "Why did they ever have to get old? Mama, I'm here. I'm grown up."

There is no good place for the last two roses. I put them on the asphalt where the dining room table was. Tomorrow someone will run over them in the parking lot. But who would disturb them today?

89
_____

A Return
to Christmases Gone